Bats

Phil Richardson

FIREFLY BOOKS

For Jalna

A Firefly Book

Published by Firefly Books Ltd. 2011

First printing

Publisher Cataloging-in-Publication Data (U.S.)

Richardson, Phil.
  Bats / Phil Richardson.
[128] p. : ill., col. photos., maps ; cm.
Includes index.
Summary: A guided tour of the nocturnal world of bats: where
they live, how they feed, their complex life cycles, and how they
survive in almost every habitat. Includes ways to watch and
study bats, as well as and ways to help in their conservation.
ISBN-13: 978-1-55407-803-5 (pbk.)
ISBN-10: 1-55407-803-2 (pbk.)
1. Bats. I. Title.
599.4 dc22   QL737.C5R5343 2011

Library and Archives Canada Cataloguing in Publication

Richardson, Phil
            Bats / Phil Richardson.
Includes index.
ISBN-13: 978-1-55407-803-5
ISBN-10: 1-55407-803-2
      1. Bats. 2. Bats—Conservation. I. Title.
QL737.C5R53 2011   599.4   C2010-905613-2

Published in the United States by
Firefly Books (U.S.) Inc.
P.O. Box 1338, Ellicott Station
Buffalo, New York 14205

Published in Canada by
Firefly Books Ltd.
66 Leek Crescent
Richmond Hill, Ontario L4B 1H1

Printed in China by C & C Offset Printing Co.,Ltd.

Developed by:
the Natural History Museum
Cromwell Road, London SW7 5BD

For the Natural History Museum:
Edited by Jonathan Elphick
Designed by Mercer Design, London
Reproduction by Saxon Digital
Services

Front cover image: © Carsten Braun

Contents

Preface

O F THE WORLD'S OVER 5,000 SPECIES of mammals, more than 1,100 – one in five – are bats. They vary in size from amazingly tiny, almost butterfly-sized creatures, to huge animals with wingspans of nearly 2 m (6 ft 7 in). Thanks to their mastery of powered flight, bats are distributed across much of the world. They feed mainly on insects and fruits, but some eat nectar, frogs, fish or even other small mammals or blood.

Everyone reacts to bats, sometimes with horror but nowadays more with fascination. Although they are linked in many people's minds with horror films, the truth about these amazing creatures' real lives is very different from the Hollywood image. This book goes behind the scenes and reveals that bats have a complex lifestyle, a rich social life and senses that are almost beyond our comprehension. In wildlife books there is always a tendency to show images of the biggest, the prettiest, the fastest, the most bizarre-looking and so on. In the case of bats, it seems that every species that has been studied has at least one remarkable feature associated with it, and the more research is carried out, the more fascinating details emerge.

In this book we look at a cross-section of the species that have fitted so well into the environment – where they live, how they feed and breed, and the special features that they have evolved for various purposes (many of which we still do not fully understand). Bats have an important role to play in the natural world around us. The fruit eating species are major seed dispersers, while the nectar feeders are pollinators of trees and plants in tropical areas, and have been found to be of importance in regenerating areas of cleared tropical forest. Insect eaters maintain the famous balance of nature, preying on huge numbers of flying insects every night, some of which can become serious pests of our crops, farm animals, buildings and ourselves.

AUTHOR

Phil Richardson, once a science teacher by day, but now a bat ecologist, spends days, nights and holidays working with bats. He helped popularize bats in the UK by making them appealing to the public in TV and radio presentations, and in the setting up of a number of volunteer bat groups and the Bat Conservation Trust, the UK national body involved in bat conservation. He is the author of another popular book on this group of animals, *Bats* (2000).

OPPOSITE One of around 1,100 species of bats, the long-eared bat, *Plecotus auritus*, drinking from a pool.

CHAPTER 1

Bat evolution and biology

MAMMALS HAVE BEEN in existence for over 200 million years, but began to diversify greatly around 65 million years ago. The earliest fossil insect-eating bat found to date is 50 million years old and is very similar to the species of bats that exist today, indicating that they had already largely evolved. Perhaps the major part of bats' evolution occurred 70 or more million years ago. There were important influences at this time: flowering plants had also diversified between 70 and 100 million years ago, providing new foods for insects and other animals, and the rulers of the world, the dinosaurs, had died out by 65 million years ago. The mammals that began appearing on the scene were different, they had hair on their body instead of scales, gave birth to live young rather than laying eggs, and provided their young with milk from special glands.

Unfortunately no 'missing links' have yet been found to show clearly the bats' evolutionary route; their bones are very thin and fragile, so bat fossils are rare. The most likely suggestion is that they evolved from a shrew-like mammal that climbed trees, apart from the large group known as fruit bats, which seem to have had a different origin. The earliest known fossil of a fruit bat is only 35 million years old. Although fruit bats appear superficially similar to insect-eating bats, they are very different in a number of ways, such as the shape of their skulls and teeth, their neck vertebrae and the bones in their hands. It is likely that they evolved along a very different path from the insectivorous bats, one

that branched off from the primates, the group that contains monkeys, apes and humans. It is possible, therefore, that these bats are distantly related to us.

OPPOSITE Lesser long-nosed bat, *Leptonycteris curasoae yerbabuenae*, and Parry's century plant (*Agave parryi*) flower stalk. These bats are specialized for visiting flowers and feeding on nectar and pollen. They have elongated rostrums, long, brush-tipped tongues, reduced tooth number and size, and the ability to subsist on a diet of nectar and pollen. They spend spring and summer in the southwestern USA, then migrate to central Mexico for the rest of the year.

LEFT A fossil microbat, *Palaeochiropteryx tupaiodon*, from the Messel deposits in Germany over 45 million years old, but very similar to present-day bats.

CLASSIFICATION OF BATS

ABOVE The Solomons bare-backed fruit bat, *Dobsonia inermis*, is one of about 186 species of megabats.

As with other living things, biologists find it convenient to group similar species of bats together into a genus (plural: genera) and then group similar genera into families. The families are then grouped into sub-orders and then into an order. The order that incorporates all bats has the Latin name Chiroptera, which means 'hand-wing'. This is made up of two sub-orders, the Megachiroptera (popularly known as megabats) and the Microchiroptera (or microbats).

There is only one family of megabats, that of the Old World fruit bats, and it includes approximately 186 species. Species belonging to the most diverse genus *Pteropus*, which make up over one-third of all the megabats, are called flying foxes. Although many megabats are big, as the name suggests, the Megachiroptera also includes a large number of species that are smaller than some of the microbats. As their name suggests, most if not all of the Old World fruit bats feed on fruit, though for some, pollen and nectar may be more important in the diet and members of the genus *Nyctimene* may take some insects.

The approximately 930 species of microbats are grouped into 17 families. Again, the popular name of the sub-order can be misleading. Some of the microbats are large, with impressive wingspans, though none is as big as the largest megabats. Although most are insect-eaters, by no means all of them are, and the range of diets is very wide.

The 'local' name for a species may be completely different from the name given to the same bat in a neighbouring country. Each species is, therefore, given a Latinized scientific name to try to avoid such confusions. This consists of two parts: the first word, the generic name (which always has an initial capital), refers to the genus and the second, or specific name, indicates the particular species within that genus. In many cases, species are further divided into sub-species, or geographical races, involving a third name. The words used are often descriptive, so *Myotis macrotarsus* means 'mouse-eared bat with big feet'. Some species, such as *M. daubentonii*, are named after people (Daubenton was a French naturalist) and some, such as *M. atacamensis*, for a species found in the Atacama desert, after geographical regions.

As one would expect, new species are being discovered occasionally in remote areas of rainforest or on isolated oceanic islands, but recently a new species was found in Britain, a country where bats are watched relatively intensively. The pipistrelle, the smallest European bat, and the commonest species in Britain, was formerly regarded as a single species, *Pipistrellus pipistrellus*.

ABOVE The common pipistrelle, *Pipistrellus pipistrellus*, is one of about 930 species of microbats.

CLASSIFICATION OF BATS

This bat has been studied for decades, but it was not until the 1990s that bat researchers realized that there are actually two different species. If a new species can be found in Britain, then it is likely there are other species in other parts of the world just waiting to be discovered.

So the total number of species worldwide is always changing, as new ones are discovered and as others become extinct. Another reason for the total frequently being altered is that different taxonomists decide to 'split' one species into two, or 'lump' two into one. An example is that of the round-eared tube-nosed bat, *Nyctimene cyclotis*, of New Guinea that was thought to have a sub-species, *Nyctimene cyclotis certans*; now some taxonomists think that this is really a full species, *Nyctimene certans*.

CHIROPTERA

MEGACHIROPTERA – THE MEGABATS

Family (scientific name)	Family (common name)	Approximate no. of genera	Approximate no. of species
Pteropodidae	Old World fruit bats	42	186

MICROCHIROPTERA – THE MICROBATS

Family (scientific name)	Family (common name)	Approximate no. of genera	Approximate no. of species
Rhinopomatidae	Mouse-tailed bats	1	4
Emballonuridae	Sheath-tailed, sac-winged, pouched, and ghost bats	13	51
Craseonycteridae	Hog-nosed bat	1	1
Nycteridae	Slit-faced bats	1	16
Megadermatidae	False vampire and yellow-winged bats	4	5
Rhinolophidae	Horseshoe bats	1	77
Hipposideridae	Old World leaf-nosed bats	9	81
Noctilionidae	Bulldog or fisherman bats	1	2
Mormoopidae	Naked-backed, moustached, and ghost-faced bats	2	10
Phyllostomidae	New World leaf-nosed bats	55	160
Natalidae	Funnel-eared bats	3	8
Furipteridae	Smoky bats	2	2
Thyropteridae	Disc-winged bats	1	3
Myzopodidae	Sucker-footed bats	1	1
Vespertilionidae	Vesper bats	48	407
Mystacinidae	New Zealand short-tailed bats	1	2 (1 extinct)
Molossidae	Free-tailed or mastiff bats	16	100

BELOW Representatives of the world's bat families.

Pteropodidae
Egyptian rousette

Rhinopomatidae
Greater mouse-tailed bat

Emballonuridae
Sac-winged bat

Craseonycteridae
Hog-nosed bat

Nycteridae
Egyptian slit-faced bat

Megadermatidae
Yellow-winged bat

Rhinolophidae
Lesser horseshoe bat

Hipposideridae
Diadem leaf-nosed bat

Noctilionidae
Fisherman bat

Mormoopidae
Davy's naked-backed bat

Pyllostomidae
Tent-building bat

Natalidae
Mexican funnel-eared bat

Furipteridae
Eastern smoky bat

Thyropteridae
Spix's disc-winged bat

Myzopodidae
Sucker-footed bat

Vespertilionidae
Big brown bat

Mystacinidae
New Zealand lesser short-tailed bat

Molossidae
Brazilian free-tailed bat

PRESENT DIVERSITY

Flight gives bats the opportunity to go almost anywhere. Mountain ranges, seas or similar barriers that are obstacles to land-based mammals restrict them far less. Bats have been able to reach isolated islands in vast oceans and to cross continents. Having arrived, they are affected by their new environment. Pressures of food, shelter and predators all have an influence. Over millions of years some failed to survive, but others adapted and flourished. After many, many generations, these survivors gradually changed by the process of natural selection into new species. Today's 1,100-odd species of bats live in habitats as diverse as deserts, riversides, forests and even cities. There have been records of bats as high as 5,000 m (16,400 ft). Some bats have increased the range of food taken from insects and fruit to include nectar, fish, amphibians, birds, small mammals and even blood. Where there's a suitable niche, there's generally a bat to occupy it.

BELOW A parti-coloured bat, *Vespertilio murinus*, flying from its roost with its mouth open for echolocation. This is one of the 407 species in the largest bat family, the Vespertilionidae.

BAT DISTRIBUTION

Bats are found in many parts of the world in most terrestrial habitats, except in colder parts of the northern and southern hemispheres beyond the limit of tree growth or on some oceanic islands. The number of species increases towards the equator, where there is more available food of more varied types than in temperate regions. Thus about 120 species occur in the northern part of South America, but only 45 or so in the whole of North America. Some regions have a particularly great diversity, for instance, approximately 100 species of bats are found in Southeast Asia, but only about 60 in central Africa and a similar number in Australia. Fewer species are found on small islands than on larger continents, so Europe as a whole has about 30, Britain 16 and Ireland only seven species.

Each species is restricted in its range due to the niche it has filled, governed by food, temperature and roosting site availability. Some species have an extensive range, particularly those on large land masses. For example, Daubenton's bat, *Myotis daubentonii*, is found throughout Europe and eastwards as far as Japan. The range of the hoary bat, *Lasiurus cinereus*, extends from Canada south to Chile and Argentina. Schreibers' bent-winged bat, *Miniopterus schreibersii*, occurs from southern Europe to southern Africa, and east to Japan and South Australia.

Other species, by contrast, have very small ranges. A number of the flying foxes are restricted to a few tropical islands in the middle of oceans, such as the Rodrigues fruit bat, *Pteropus rodricensis*, which is found only on the island of Rodrigues in the Indian Ocean. The Fijian monkey-faced bat, *Pteralopex acrodonta*, is only found on the island of Taveuni in Fiji, and only in montane forest on the summit of one small mountainous area. Among the microbats, Kitti's hog-nosed bat, *Craseonycteris thonglongyai*, is found only in a few caves on the Thai-Burmese border.

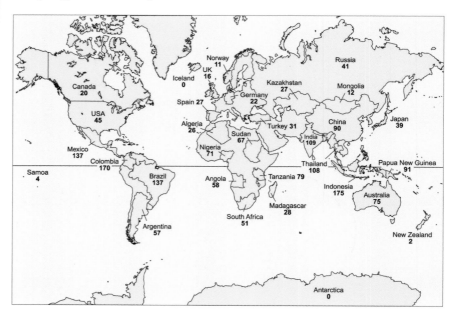

RIGHT The map shows the distribution of species in some countries, with greater numbers of species towards the equator and on large landmasses.

BAT STRUCTURE

Bat bones are relatively thin and light to help with the problem of weight and flight. Flight requires plenty of energy so the lighter the bones, the better. A bat that was as heavy as a similar sized non-flying mammal would not only need to have incredibly strong flight muscles, but would be using up energy at a very rapid rate, probably faster than it could supply it, just to counteract the downward pull of gravity. The comparative lightness of bats means that they are manoeuvrable and agile in the air.

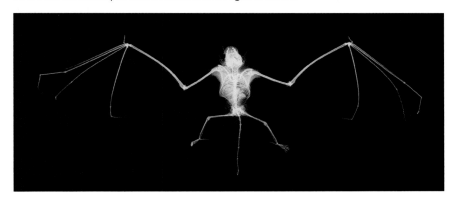

LEFT This X-ray shows a bat's long fingers and outwardly bending knees.

WINGS AND LEGS

Two other major differences between the skeletons of bats and those of other mammals are the structure of the wings and the legs. The wings are the most remarkable feature of bats. Like humans, they have four fingers and a thumb on each

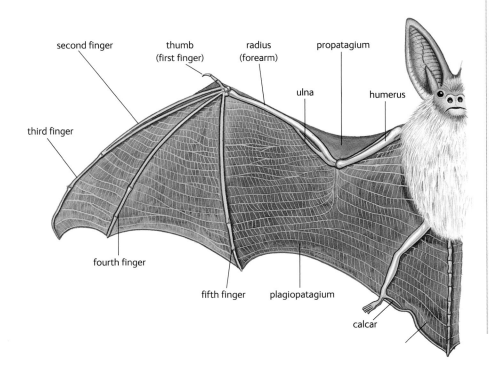

second finger

thumb (first finger)

radius (forearm)

propatagium

ulna

humerus

third finger

fourth finger

fifth finger

plagiopatagium

calcar

LEFT The structure of a bat showing the key features of the wings and legs.

hand, but the fingers are very long, each about as long as the body, and very thin. The thumb is relatively small and has a claw that is used for gripping when the bat is at rest, whereas the fingers have lost their claws (except in many fruit bats of the Old World, which have a claw on their second finger).

The legs are attached so that the knees bend the opposite way to those of humans, backwards and outwards instead of forwards. This enables bats to move more rapidly on all fours across a surface such as a cave roof, rather like a spider. It also helps them to squeeze quickly into narrow crevices to escape predators. For those species with a tail membrane, backward-flexing knees enable them to move the attached membrane downwards in flight to aid food catching and aerial manoeuvring.

FOREARMS

When at rest, a bat holds its forearms along the sides of its body. The forearm can be measured easily and its length is used widely to help identify different species. Forearm length is a very good guide to the size of the whole bat. A very small bat has a forearm that is 3 cm (1.2 in) long, whereas very large bats have forearms as long as 15 cm (6 in). A couple of millimetres may not sound much, but they represent a noticeable difference to the size of the whole bat; a bat with a 4 cm (1.6 in) forearm looks much bigger than one with a forearm measuring 3.7 cm (1.5 in).

RIGHT Measuring the forearm length is a useful guide to the size of a bat.

SKULL

The skull of any mammal always reveals much about how the animal lives, and so it is with bats. Apart from fruit bats, all bats have the skull attached to the spine by special vertebrae that enable them to bend their necks backwards, so that they can hang straight down in a roost and arch their heads back to look around. The teeth of insect-eating bats have sharp spiky edges so that the upper and lower jaws work rather like scissors and can chop up the hard outer-body casings of insects. The front teeth are usually very small to prevent interference with their echolocation pulses (see p.26). Fruit bats have flatter molars that work better when mashing the pulp of fruit. Unusual dentition will indicate specialist feeding methods, for example vampire bats have specially designed incisors and canines with razor sharp edges to enable them to slice into skin with as little sensation to the prey as possible. The skull also reflects some special features of a bat's head, so, for example, the horseshoe bats have a raised lump of bone on the top of the snout of the skull that coincides with the fleshy nose leaf on the face.

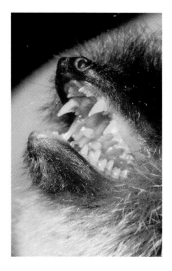

ABOVE The teeth of microbats usually have very sharp edges for cutting up their insect prey. The incisors themselves are tiny.

TOP LEFT The skull of a megabat measuring 7 cm (2.75 in). The long snout helps it smell out fruit, the flattened molars are for crushing it, and its large eye sockets contain big eyes for good vision in the dark.

LEFT The skull of a microbat measuring 4 cm (1.6 in), with its relatively short snout and lower jaw.

FLIGHT

Humans have tiny flaps of skin joining the bases of their fingers. Bats have a much, much larger double-thick membrane of skin, called the patagium, that joins their long fingers from the bases to the tips. The fingers cannot be flexed independently, but muscles in the arm can open up the hand, so producing a wing, rather like opening up an umbrella, where the spokes of the umbrella give the cloth covering strength and shape. The surface area is made even larger by the main inner part of the membrane, the plagiopatagium, joining to the side of the bat's body and all the way down to the legs. The human equivalent would be to have thin, spindly fingers 2 m (6 ft 7 in) long stretching out from your hands and covered in material that also reached from the side of your arm and hand down to your ankle, joining up to your leg and the side of your body. It would limit your activities greatly, as you could no longer use your hands for gripping, pushing or levering. Stretch out your arms and fingers, however, and you have a massive surface area that, if flapped up and down with sufficient force, could give you lift.

A long fifth finger results in a wide wing, usually associated with a short wing too, and this is useful for a hovering, very manoeuvrable flight that is ideal when hunting in a cluttered environment such as in forest. A long, narrow wing enables a fast flight and this is common amongst species that travel some distance from their roosting places to foraging sites. Different species have evolved different wing shapes to fit with their foraging preferences and life styles.

The large skin area of the wing also allows for a certain amount of gliding, albeit for short periods of time, but both megabats and microbats can be seen at times to glide around between flaps on outstretched wings. The energy needed for a bat to fly is enormous. To power its flight muscles a bat's heart-rate goes up from about 300 beats a minute at rest to 1,000 beats a minute in flight. The curved surface of a bat's wing provides lift, if it is moving forward fast enough. On

BELOW The rubbery skin of the wing membranes of this long-eared bat, *Plecotus*, occupies a large area, and joins to the legs. It is criss-crossed with blood vessels.

the upstroke the wing partially folds, so that it is easier to raise and does not push the bat downwards, but it regains its shape on the downstroke. The leading edge has a flap of skin, the propatagium, that can be adjusted to prevent stalling when manoeuvring. Leg and arm movements can adjust the surface area and shape of the wings to allow turns, banking and deceleration. Bats can even use a wing to catch a flying insect and transfer it into their mouths in flight. Having solid skin covering the wing enables a bat to carry out sudden changes of direction, whereas the 'leaky' feathers of a bird's wing may allow air to pass through, causing the bird to drift when it tries to change direction suddenly.

There are tiny bumps, each with a tiny hair, on the wings' surfaces, and recent research has indicated that these are sensitive to touch, and can detect changes in air pressure. This enables a bat to fine-tune its flight performance by sensing the pressure changes on different parts of the wing as it carries out various manoeuvres, and so enables the bat to adjust the various profiles of the wings for maximum performance.

When not used for flying the wings of many families of bats are folded carefully at their sides, and in the case of an endemic New Zealand bat folded beneath thick protective rubbery skin at the sides of the bat for extra protection, as it spends a lot of time running around on the ground foraging for insects, and tunnelling into dead wood. In the case of megabats and a few families of microbats, the wings at rest are wrapped around the body like a cloak, so giving some measure of protection against adverse environmental conditions. Some megabats even have cryptic patterning on their wings so when covering the body they merge into the background of their roosting place.

The bare-faced fruit bats, *Dobsonia* spp., have wing membranes continuing across the back, with the usual body fur beneath. This extra membrane makes this a noisy family of bats in flight as it creates a characteristic 'pok pok pok' sound whilst flying. The air pressure in this extra pocket makes the wings clap together on the upstroke. At the beginning of the down-stroke there is a sudden pressure decrease on the upper surface of the wings, so giving extra lift. This makes this bat very agile in flight and it can hover and even fly backwards, used to great effect when searching for food in a tree canopy.

Also, with wings made of skin, any damage generally heals quickly. The flight membranes are criss-crossed with tiny blood vessels to keep each area of skin healthy. Bats carefully groom their wings to keep the skin in good condition, using oils secreted from glands to help, rather like using hand cream after washing one's hands.

Flight by bats has to be powerful, since their mass changes significantly at different times in their lives. After hibernation a small female *Myotis* bat may weigh 7 g (0.24 oz), but when about to give birth, she may have increased this to 14 g (0.48 oz), and has to be able to fly with this extra weight. After the birth, a female may need to carry her youngster around, which may be well over half its mother's weight. After only a couple of hours feeding, a bat's increase in mass can be well over 50%, and fruit bats may fly off with a heavy fruit in their jaws.

TAIL MEMBRANES

Many microbat families have a full membrane of skin, the interfemoral membrane, joining their back legs and completely enclosing the tail. It is used in flight to brake and change direction, but perhaps its major use is related to feeding. As the bats are flying with their hands, they cannot use them effectively to grab a flying insect that they encounter. Instead they fly over the prey and curl down their tail to form a catching device. Still in flight, the bat can then curl its head and neck down and transfer the insect to its mouth. The bat then eats it as it flies along. There is a strengthening sliver of cartilage along the trailing edge of the membrane joined to the feet, rather like a thin sixth toe, called the calcar. Where extra strength is required in some species, such as the fishing bat, *Noctilio leporinus*, this can stretch along most of the trailing edge of the tail membrane.

RIGHT Dorsal view of the wing of the short-nosed fruit bat, *Cynopterus sphinx*. Thin finger bones support the wing membrane.

BELOW RIGHT The interfemoral membrane of a vesper bat. The rubbery skin encloses the tail and is strengthened by the bony calcar.

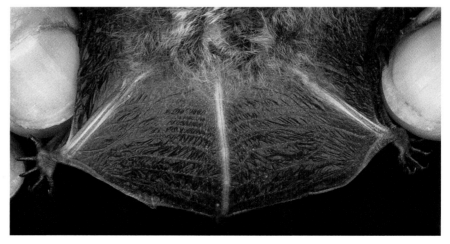

GET A GRIP!

With their front limbs highly modified for flight, most bats find moving around on the ground difficult. They can support the front of their bodies on their wrists, but have no fingers to grip with, or paws equipped with pads to soften their progress. When not flying, bats tend to rest by hanging from high places. In that way they can drop down and gain some speed to make it easier to fly off again. To facilitate hanging, they have well-developed curved claws on their toes that they hook around a branch or other suitable surface. The tips of the claws are very sharp, so bats can obtain a grip on some of the smoothest surfaces. The toes can be spread to enable the claws to grip at different angles to improve their purchase. In larger species, the claws can be hooked right around a branch.

An extremely neat adaptation is the arrangement of the ligaments and muscles in the leg which, when relaxed, keep the foot in the clenched position. This means

LEFT The thumb and claw of a bat are used for holding on firmly in the roost and gripping food items when eating.

RIGHT A greater horseshoe bat, *Rhinolophus ferrumequinum*, hibernating. The curved toes and claws grip tightly even when the bat is in a deep sleep.

that the bats can fall asleep and not drop off, rather like hanging down beneath a grappling iron. It takes the bat some effort to open its foot and release its grip, the opposite way to how our hands work. The feet support the weight of the bat, but some species also use the single claw on their thumbs to improve the grip, so ensuring that their whole body is in contact with the roosting surface. Bats also use their thumb claws to hang from when giving birth and in some species when urinating and defecating. When out feeding, fruit bats may land briefly on a tree branch in order to pluck off a fruit or feed on nectar from a flower, and at such times they use their thumbs to grip the branch. They also use them to help manipulate large food items into the mouth. Most megabats have a second claw on the second finger, but this is smaller and not really functional.

A COAT OF FUR

All mammals have hair on their bodies, although it may be sparse in the case of whales and a few other mammals. The body of a bat has a dense covering of fur that in some species spreads out onto part of the wing and tail membranes. For many species living in the temperate areas of the world warm fur is essential, to insulate them against the cold. It also serves well as body protection, particularly for those bats that squeeze their delicate little bodies into narrow, rough crevices to roost.

The individual hairs are unusual in appearance when viewed under a microscope, each having jagged edges and looking rather like a stack of miniature paper cups with uneven rims. As yet the exact function of this unusual structure is not known.

Most species have brown or black fur, often paler beneath, but there are a few oddities amongst bats. Some are almost naked and others are bright orange or all-white, or have coloured patches and stripes in their fur or frosted tips to the hairs. It may seem odd for bats, which are usually active only at night, to have coloured fur, but it seems to be restricted to species that roost outside in daytime, in which it probably has a camouflaging effect. Even the few species such as the little Central American, *Ectophylla alba*, that have all-white fur, look greenish when hanging beneath large green leaves.

Around a bat's mouth, feet and tail membranes there are special touch-sensitive hairs (whiskers and bristles) that help it catch its food. The faster-flying bats have sleek fur and those feeding close to water have a dense, waterproof fur.

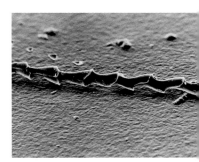

ABOVE An electron microscope view of a bat hair showing the jagged edges typical of all bats.

LEFT The dense fur of bats, such as this Brandt's bat, *Myotis brandtii*, insulates and protects its owner.

SENSES: FAMILIAR AND UNFAMILIAR

Bats are active mainly at night and their senses reflect this. They have an array of senses that they use to determine where they are going, to avoid obstacles, find food and mates, return to their roosts, and so on. As well as the familiar ones of vision, smell and hearing, these include the remarkable sense of echolocation, developed in the microbats for finding their way about and hunting insects in the darkness of night.

RIGHT A headful of senses on a microbat Schneider's leaf-nosed bat, *Hipposideros speoris*. The small eyes are typical of the microbats. The large ears and complex nose-leaf are linked to echolocation. Touch-sensitive hairs can be seen around the face.

SIGHT

Old World fruit bats have relatively large eyes with good light-gathering capacity. They need to be able to see where they are and to avoid obstacles when flying across a landscape, where the trees are that hold their fruit, and where they can perch safely when eating it. Insect-eating bats, on the other hand, have small eyes, as they use the special sense of echolocation (see p.26) for finding their food. However, they still use their eyesight for avoiding large objects, gauging their height above the ground and finding their way across a landscape by navigating visually, using prominent landmarks. Although not as well developed as a fruit bat's eyesight, their vision is particularly sensitive to low light conditions.

BELOW Large, light-gathering eyes help this megabat, *Dobsonia inermis*, to see in dark conditions. The long snout helps it to smell fruits from some distance.

Even on the darkest night there is some light around and all bats use this. Old World fruit bats have colour vision, which is useful to them as they are often quite active in daytime when roosting on trees in exposed positions, rather than tucked away in dark crevices like most microbats, which can see only in black and white.

OLFACTION: THE SENSE OF SMELL

All bats have a good sense of smell. Old World fruit bats rely on it greatly to find their food supplies, and their long muzzles are packed with smell-sensors. They are able to detect the smell of rotting fruit or the scent of a flower downwind over a considerable distance. Bats also use smell to identify their own youngsters from a crèche of apparently identical babies, often in pitch-black conditions. They have scent glands that they use to mark themselves and other members of their colony, and probably also their roosting sites. Many of these scents are odourless to us, with our poor sense of smell, although some bats have a musky smell that we can detect.

ECHOLOCATION AND HEARING

Echolocation is a type of sonar that microbats use to detect prey, locate roosting crevices and avoid close obstacles in the dark. These bats emit a very loud and short 'shout' of sound and listen for the echo that bounces back when it hits an object. Put simply, this can tell the bats how far away the object is by estimating the time it takes before they hear the echo. The longer it takes the echo to return, the farther away the object.

Although there may only be a fraction of a second's delay between shouting and hearing the echo, bats have the mental equipment to process the information. A hard-bodied insect produces a different quality of echo from one with a soft body, so bats can distinguish between some groups of insects in this way. They can also determine the size of the object.

To gain maximum information, the bats usually shout out very high-frequency sounds, usually between 20 and 200 kHz. (Humans can hear only up to 20 kHz; a dog-whistle is about 25 kHz.) High-frequency sounds have short wavelengths, which give a far more detailed echo, rather like the detail you would see on a painting produced with a fine paint brush, compared with one done using a huge decorator's brush. Bats gain even more information by giving out shouts that vary in frequency, starting off very high and sweeping down to a lower frequency.

These echolocation pulses last only a few thousandths of a second and bats emit perhaps ten or 15 calls each second. The silences between enable them to listen in to the echo information coming back. Their specially evolved brains enable them to build up an amazingly accurate picture of objects close to them. From the variable echoes produced, they can work out the size and hardness of the body of the insect.

A bat can also discern the flutter of the prey's wings and there is evidence that some bats can compute their flight speed compared with objects around them by using Doppler shift. This is the change in pitch of sound produced by a moving object. We hear, for example, the higher-pitched sound as a high-speed train approaches our platform (the approaching sound waves are compressed) and then we can detect the lowering in pitch as the train passes and races away from us (the waves are now stretched).

Using all this information means that a bat can identify and locate its prey from a distance and then attack. As it flies closer, it speeds up the echolocation calls until

ABOVE A Geoffroy's bat, *Myotis emarginatus*, hunting spiders. The echolocation calls emitted from its mouth are even able to detect the prey's fine webs.

just before contact, when they are so fast they become like a continuous trill or buzz. The information is constantly fed back to take into account any changes in direction of the prey. Experiments have shown that bats can avoid wires as fine as human hairs stretched across their flight path in pitch-black rooms.

For echolocation to work most bats have to really bellow the sound out, after all they are trying to hear the echo bouncing back from a relatively tiny, fairly soft object. Some bats produce sounds louder than 110 decibels, the same volume as a jet plane when flying low overhead. To cope with this, they have a special muscle that closes off the inside of the ear when they shout, so that they are not deafened. Fortunately, the high-frequency sounds used, although very loud, are above our sense of hearing. Bats obtain most of the energy to produce their bursts of sound 'for free' because they link their shouts to their wing-beats; they exhale and shout on every wing-stroke.

A limitation of echolocation is likely to be the range at which it can operate. High frequencies have a short range, of about 6 m (20 ft) at the most for a small bat that shouts loudly, and perhaps less than 3 m (10 ft) when a small insect is to be detected. If bats were to use low-frequency sounds instead, then the range would be much greater, but the detail would be lost. Some bats emit these sounds not through their mouths, but via their specially modified nostrils, using strange folds of skin around the nose to direct the sound waves, like people cupping their hands around their mouth before shouting.

Fruit bats of the Old World do not normally need to echolocate, because they use their keen sense of smell to locate their food, but a few, such as *Rousettus*, roost in caves and so need to find their way about in the dark. They give out a series of clicks with their tongues and echolocate as the sounds bounce back from the cave walls (see also p.49).

The hearing of bats is very sensitive to the faint, high-frequency echoes that are reflected back from tiny insects. Even the chatter bats make in roosts, which is audible to humans, has a great deal of high-frequency sound (or ultrasound) in it that we cannot hear. Lower-pitched sounds that we can hear would be inaudible or barely audible to bats. Some bats find their food by listening to the slight sounds the prey makes, the rustle of a scorpion moving across sand, the whisper of a moth's wings or the movement of a leaf caused by a passing spider.

Many bats have large ears so as to gather as much sound as possible. Generally the bigger the ears, the quieter are the bats' echolocation calls. Many insectivorous bats have an extra spike of cartilage, called a tragus, sticking up from the base of each ear and researchers think that this helps to give better sound definition in a particular plane, although, as with so many aspects involving bats, its precise function is unknown. It is certainly a useful feature for bat researchers as different species of bats have a differently shaped tragus, so its appearance can be used to identify species.

LEFT The tent-building bat, *Uroderma bilobatum*, has special folds of skin around the nostrils that are linked to sound emission, and a prominent tragus.

BAT DETECTORS

Bat calls are of a frequency too high for us to hear, but the electronics of a bat detector can convert the sounds so we can hear them. Different bat species tend to feed on different insects in different habitats in different ways and it has been found that their calls are distinguishable with a bat detector. We can listen to the bat flying by and tell what species it is.

The calls vary in repetition rate, intensity, frequency and length. As with bird song, it takes some practice to be able to distinguish the more similar species, but bat detectors are now one of the main tools of bat researchers. They are useful for obtaining accurate counts of emerging bats from a roost, as the failing light can mean that some bats are missed visually, but every bat calls as it emerges so can be heard as well as seen. When bats are approaching an insect they speed up their echolocation pulses, culminating in a trill or a buzz. These pulses can be heard on the detector and give an indication of the success rate of feeding.

Bat detectors are also now widely used by bat researchers for surveying a habitat for bats by walking along transects (sample strips crossing the habitat) and counting the bats that are heard to pass. The detectors can operate in three ways. The heterodyne approach uses a low-frequency sound made by the machine that interferes with the high-frequency calls of the bat, resulting in sound that can be heard by humans. Although it isn't the actual call that can be heard, it has the same patterns of call length, frequency and volume.

The time expansion method records part of the bat call, then plays it back more slowly. This lowers the frequency down to our audible range, just like slowing down a tape or a record causes the sound to drop in pitch. This method retains all the information of the call and is widely used for detailed analysis using computer software. The third approach is the frequency division technique, in which the detector takes every tenth sound wave, so reducing the sound in frequency to our range of hearing. Each method has its advantages and disadvantages, so one may be used for precise species identification and another for sampling bats in a habitat. Whichever type is used, it opens one's eyes, and ears, to another world.

BELOW LEFT Calls of Daubenton's bat, *Myotis daubentonii*, sweep down from high to a lower frequency every $^4/_{100}$ths of a second. The second sweep in each pair is the echo off the water surface.

BELOW Calls of a Darling's horseshoe bat, *Rhinolophus darlingi*, are at an almost fixed frequency, and repeated every $^1/_{10}$th of a second.

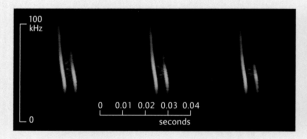

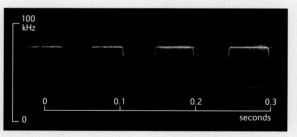

HOW ECHOLOCATION WORKS

This specific example should help you to understand how echolocation works. Imagine a bat shouting towards a moth 2 m (6 ft 7 in) away in front of a tree 8 m (26 ft 3 in) away from it.

● **THE SHOUT** The bat gives out a short, loud shout. It lasts for about 2 ms (2 milliseconds is 2/1,000ths of a second). Like any other sound in air under normal conditions it travels at about 340 m/second (765 mph), so that this 'click' of sound is a wedge about 68 cm (27 in) thick. Each bat shout sweeps down from a very high frequency to a lower one, so the front of the wedge will be the higher frequencies and the back will be the lower ones. After shouting, the bat's contracted ear muscles relax and the now sensitive ears await any echoes.

- **THE MOTH'S ECHO** The sound wedge reaches the flying moth 2m (6ft 7in) away after 6ms and part of the thick wall of sound will be reflected. The rest of the wedge continues on towards the tree. The front of the echo from the moth starts arriving back at the ears 12ms after the shout and the rest of it has been heard by 14ms. The bat will now have a three-dimensional sound image of the moth and, from the time delay of the echo, can compute its distance.

- **THE TREE'S ECHO** The shout begins arriving at the tree after 24ms and a tree-shaped echo is produced. This returns to the bat, and hits the moth a second time from the back and a moth-shaped shadow is produced in the middle. This echo arrives back between 48 and 50ms after the shout. The tree echo may not have as much detail as the moth echo because higher-frequency sounds have less range, so the first sounds back (those of higher frequency) may be too quiet to be heard. The moth's echo stands out against its shadow in the second echo and will be louder than the echo of the tree, which appears as a fainter background. With all the information gathered after a mere 5/100th of a second, it is now time to shout again.

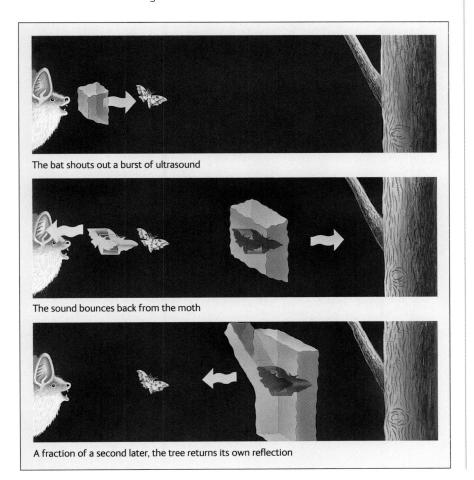

The bat shouts out a burst of ultrasound

The sound bounces back from the moth

A fraction of a second later, the tree returns its own reflection

LEFT Echolocation in action, how one shout from a microbat can enable it to detect prey and the surrounding environment. The illustration is a simplified version of what happens. In reality, a bat can obtain more information by using harmonics, varying the call rate, call length, call intensity and extending the time of a constant frequency component.

CHAPTER 2
Bat behaviour

ATTEMPTING TO UNDERSTAND THE BEHAVIOUR of bats is one of the most fascinating and challenging aspects of research on bat biology. In many cases, the reasons why bats behave in particular ways seem obvious, but there are still a large number of bat activities that remain unexplained. Even when researchers have understood one aspect of a bat's behaviour, it is not possible to assume that a different species will behave in the same way. Although some behaviour can be looked at generally, it usually turns out that at least one species of bat does the opposite from the norm. There is enough work here to keep a roost-full of bat researchers busy for centuries.

OPPOSITE Numbers of bats at some megabat roosts, such as these *Pteropus* sp., can be so large that the trees are damaged by the weight of bats and their droppings.

ROOSTING

Animals need a place to shelter when at rest, away from extremes of temperature, rain or wind, and preferably close to their food supply. Although most bats roost during the daytime high up, some species choose lower sites, even such places as under rocks in deserts. Bats' front hands are not much use for defence from predators, having evolved into wings, and their back legs are often supporting them as they hang, so cannot be used for either kicking or scratching. Accordingly, bats generally try to find a shelter that will give them protection by being inaccessible to possible predators, although many megabats hang out in the open on tree branches. This protection may be because the location is high up or perhaps has a very narrow entrance.

The most commonly used roost sites are cavities and crevices in trees and in caves. Since humans appeared, the bats have also made use of many of our structures such as the roof spaces of buildings, walls, cellars, mines and tunnels, war-time bunkers, tombs, niches in churches, temples and other old buildings, and crevices in bridges, to serve as roosts where they can rest in safety. Whenever possible, microbats seem to choose dark sites such as those listed above. Bats spend a large proportion of their lives in their roosts, especially in temperate regions of the world, where summer days are particularly long.

In temperate areas, two major factors influencing bats in their choice of roosting places are the temperatures and humidity of the site in question. Bat embryos develop only slowly when cold, so females choose hot sites when they are pregnant. Males have relatively little need for activity in the spring and summer, so they may be found in cooler roosting sites, such as unheated church buildings and cool tunnels or caves, where they can conserve their stored energy.

Bats usually have a number of alternative roost sites to which they can move at different times of the year, enabling them to select the most suitable temperature for their particular needs. Large underground sites typically have a range of different temperatures and humidities between the entrance and the deepest part, and bats use different sections accordingly. In house roofs, though many species can cope with temperatures of 40°C (104°F), it sometimes becomes too hot even for bats, so they move deeper into the structure where it is cooler, such as into the cavity wall. In the Old World tropics, fruit bats, hanging out in the open, do not have this opportunity, and may fan themselves with their wings to cool their bodies during the hottest part of the day.

Unlike most other mammals, bats do not furnish their resting places with soft or warm material, nor do they chew at the entrance hole to enlarge it. They simply enter

BELOW The cave fruit bat, *Eonycteris spelaea*, is one of the few megabats that roosts in caves, sometimes with as many as 4,000 individuals together.

and hang themselves up. If a site does not suit them, then they move to another location. During the course of the summer in temperate areas, roosts of bats will regularly move between many different sites for reasons as yet unknown, although the changing conditions at each site must play an important part.

ABOVE Grey-headed flying foxes, *Pteropus poliocephalus*, form camps that may contain 200,000 individuals in tree branches, where they live and breed.

TYPICAL ROOST SITES

- **IN TREES** Most megabats form large gatherings, known as camps, in specially selected trees, where they hang from the upper branches. Microbats prefer to hide away and enter holes and crevices in the trunk or branches. Some hang out in the open or under leaves, but have cryptic colouring to camouflage them.
- **UNDERGROUND** In large sites, bats may hang from the highest part of the roof of a cave or other underground site, knowing that they are out of reach of predators, but in smaller sites they may squeeze into a crevice to provide protection from attack or to avoid becoming chilled by any breezes that may be blowing through a tunnel.
- **IN BUILDINGS** As with other sites, an important factor determining the choice of site is to keep out of harm's way, so bats in a roof space usually roost high up on the ridge beam, under the eaves or squeezed between the outer roof covering and any lining. Some wriggle into the cavity between the inner and outer walls, some find safety between stones or bricks where the mortar is missing, while others are even able to nestle within the expansion joints on bridges. A small bat can enter a roosting site through a gap as little as 1 cm (0.4 in) wide.

RECORD ROOSTS

In most species females gather together to produce young communally. The extreme example of this behaviour among the microbats is that of the Mexican free-tailed bat, *Tadarida brasiliensis*, whose vast congregations in some caves during the 1960s were estimated to contain as many as 50 million individuals, the largest known gatherings of any mammal.

Such mega-roosts become famous and attract tourists. In Thailand some of the roosts of wrinkle-lipped bats, *Tadarida plicata*, number about one million and have become part of the tourist guides' itinerary. In America, the largest roosts of Mexican free-tailed bats, *Tadarida brasiliensis*, in Texas and New Mexico still number over 5 million, even though numbers have dropped in recent years, and a whole tourist industry has been built around the phenomenon. The bats emerge at sunset in a continuous stream, looking like smoke emerging from the cave entrance. This stream stretches out to the far horizon, and still more emerge well into the night. In the morning, returning bats can also create an unforgettable spectacle as they arrive high and suddenly plunge down at breakneck speed back into their roost.

Many other species of microbats gather in much smaller numbers. A thousand is unusual as with greater mouse-eared bats, *Myotis myotis*, in Europe, a few hundred is more common as in roosts of horseshoe bats, *Rhinolophus*, and pipistrelles, *Pipistrellus*, and there are some species where usually only four or fewer individuals roost together at any one time.

Some megabats, too, gather in spectacular numbers in their camps. Little red flying foxes, *Pteropus scapulatus*, in Australia have formed gatherings containing over one million individuals. Such numbers can cause damage to the trees in which they roost from the sheer weight of the bats and their droppings.

Why do some bats gather in such huge numbers? Clustering can increase the warmth of the whole roost site. There are advantages gained from putting all the babies in one crèche, as long as it is a safe one. Certainly for bats roosting outside, more than one pair of eyes is useful for defence. Perhaps a more important benefit is that a huge number of bats emerging is likely to confuse any predators that may be waiting outside the roost. Chattering noises can often be heard where bats gather together in the daytime, so communication may be another important reason to gather. Those bat species that don't form large roosts must find alternative benefits from roosting in smaller numbers.

NIGHT ROOSTS

Bats also use night roosts, places where they can rest temporarily between feeding bouts. These may be places that are sometimes also used in the day or for winter hibernation. In some instances, they may even be sited out in the open, for example on the trunk of a tree, where the bats use the dark of the night to hide.

LOCATING ROOSTS

Finding roosts can be difficult, but many species of microbats swarm around their roost sites when returning in the early morning before entering, and this activity is very obvious and visible. With Old World fruit bats, locating roosts is generally much easier. All the investigator has to do is to follow his or her nose. Large camps of fruit bats can be remarkably pungent.

HIBERNATION AND HIBERNACULA

In temperate areas of the world, the cold weather typical of the winter months results in few insects being available to sustain the microbats. To cope with this seasonal

OPPOSITE These flying foxes set off from the day roost at dusk to forage in the surrounding forest.

ABOVE Bat researchers searching for hibernating bats tucked into rock crevices in a mine.

famine, the bats are able to hibernate. They can survive for months in this state just on the stores of fat they have already built up in their bodies. As with their summer roosts, they choose their winter roosting places, called hibernacula, to provide the optimum environment for their hibernation.

Different species choose slightly different conditions, but the temperature is generally below 10˚C (50˚F). The site must be insulated from any changes in temperature outside, so the bats often select underground sites, or crevices deep within an old tree. High humidity is also essential, as bats can easily dehydrate during hibernation.

Also, once they enter hibernation, they are defenceless against danger, as it takes half an hour or more for a bat to revert back to its normal alertness after being woken. For this reason they choose even more inaccessible places than in summer, where they may hibernate singly or form clusters. They allow their body temperatures to drop almost to that of the environment around them. If it becomes too cold, they move to another roosting site with more suitable conditions.

Microbats may swarm around a roost before entering early in the morning, but in autumn in temperate regions some have also been seen swarming around the entrance of hibernacula, flying round and round, often in relatively large numbers. As this happens before the period when the bats hibernate, it appears that their behaviour is linked to information-gathering or breeding strategies. This is yet another area of the study of bat behaviour where knowledge is lacking and there are opportunities for research.

BREEDING

In temperate areas, bats mate during the autumn or winter. Females seek out males, some of which are known to give out special calls to attract females to mate with them. Some species also probably emit scents, for the same purpose. These may be associated with special tufts of hair on the face, shoulders or other parts of the body.

MATING CALLS

Male bats give out special calls to let the females know where they are, and possibly to warn off other males. Some do this from a prominent roosting place in a tree or on the side of a building. Others fly up and down the same route, calling as they fly. The calls of microbats are often low-pitched, almost down to the range of human hearing. This means that the sound will travel further, so advertising the bat to a wider audience. Any female passing may be attracted and pay the male a visit.

The noisiest known bats are males of the hammer-headed fruit bat, *Hypsignathus monstrosus*, of Africa. They produce a series of loud, low-frequency honking calls at breeding time, not solitarily but in groups, known as leks, with other males. All the males are concentrated in a small area, trying to out-shout each other. The combined cacophony has been aptly compared to a pond full of noisy frogs. If a female ventures near, the calls become more frantic as each suitor tries to lure

her with his own sweet love song. In no other mammal has the anatomy been so modified for sound production. The males have large inflatable air-sacs housed in an elongated hammer-shaped head and a huge larynx (voice-box) almost half the length of their backbone that fills so much of the chest cavity that the heart and lungs are pushed to the back and sides.

ABOVE The bizarre-looking head of the hammer-headed fruit bat, *Hypsignathus monstrosus*, helps the males emit their remarkably loud mating calls.

ABOVE At a harem of greater spear-nosed bats, *Phyllostomus hastatus*, in Trinidad, a male stands guard over his females. The bat at top left is a vesper bat that has joined the group.

MATING

A single male may mate with 30 or more females. Sometimes, the element of choice is removed from the mating strategy because males may move around in hibernacula and mate with hibernating females. The females carry the males' live sperm inside the uterus throughout the winter months, ovulate in spring and become pregnant. This method is unusual, and few mammals other than bats use it. Some species of bats rely on delayed implantation, where the egg is produced and fertilized by the sperm, but it is not implanted in the uterus until a suitable time, often so that birth can coincide with an abundance of suitable food for the nursing mother.

The development rate of a foetus is affected by temperature, so if the mother bat stays active and chooses warm roosts the foetus will develop quickly. Development can be slowed or delayed for weeks by cold conditions. In some species, mating takes place and the egg is fertilized and implanted immediately, but development may be arrested during cold winter months. Others just get straight on with it. Fertilization comes immediately after mating, followed by the development of the embryo and birth. This approach is more common in bats living in tropical areas that are not affected as much by cold weather.

BIRTH AND DEVELOPMENT OF YOUNG

Birth occurs usually between 40 days and six months after the egg begins to develop, (usually the bigger the bat the longer the gestation period), quite a long time for such small mammals. In temperate areas many species segregate to form maternity colonies, sometimes of many hundreds of expectant females, with males roosting elsewhere, often singly. Some male microbats in tropical areas stand guard over a harem of between 10 and 100 females that roost close to him, chasing other males away if necessary.

A single baby a year is the norm for the majority of species. Some species occasionally have twins, some have twins each time, but four is the greatest number of offspring and this is unusual and restricted to a very few species, such as the red bat, *Lasiurus borealis*,

BELOW A baby Natterer's bat, *Myotis nattereri*, with its mother. It is born with large feet which are vital for clinging to the roost site and to its mother.

LIFE CYCLE

Microbats in temperate areas

Jan	Feb	Mar	Apr	May	Jun	Jul	Aug	Sept	Oct	Nov	Dec
Hibernation			Maternity roost			Birth	Young fly	Mating		Hibernation	

Female bats rarely give birth when they are one year old, but do so more commonly by the time they are two. Some species do not produce young until they have reached four years of age. Females are not usually successful in producing a youngster every year. However, a banded female bat has been found to give birth in the wild in most years during a 16-year period.

Bats in tropical areas are not limited to giving birth by cold seasons, they are only limited by rainy and dry seasons. Some bats do manage to breed twice a year.

Males do not mate until they are at least one year old, and usually not until they are two years of age or more. Although there is a high mortality rate among young bats, and the average age of a species may be only five years old, some bats have been found to live for up to 30 years in the wild.

Why is it that bats have such a long life compared with other small mammals? Producing only one young at most in a year is a very slow rate of reproduction. Long life ensures the survival of the species.

of Canada and America. In tropical areas, some bats manage to produce young twice a year, during the wet seasons, to coincide with the greatest abundance of food at these times. Usually the male-to-female ratio of babies is equal.

The birthweights of megabat babies are typically about 12% of the mother's body mass, whereas newborn microbats are about a quarter of their mothers' weight. Imagine a human female giving birth to a baby weighing 13 kg (28 lb)! The advantage of producing such heavy babies is that it does not take too long for the young to be weaned.

The babies of many species of bats are born naked and with their eyes closed, but their fur soon appears and covers their bodies, and their eyes are open within a few days. In a few species the young are born already covered with fur and with their eyes open. As with all mammals, the mother bat produces milk to feed her offspring. She usually leaves her baby in the roost when she goes off to feed at night. The babies of colonial bats are parked together in a crèche, the returning mothers identify their own offspring by going to the area where they left them and then using their sense of smell and listening for their own baby's unique squeak to locate it. Mothers are also able to carry their babies hanging onto their undersides, so can move roosts at will.

Within three weeks, the young of many microbats are almost full sized and are able to fly, assuming that the weather conditions are favourably warm for the baby to develop quickly and enable the mother to feed well to produce milk. This is another feature of bats which is very different from other mammals, as bat mothers are giving milk to nearly full-sized youngsters. As with most things related to bats, there are exceptions to the rule. Fruit bats tend to develop more slowly, for instance, while pregnancies in vampire bats last about seven months and it takes another four months before the young can fly.

FOOD AND FEEDING

Like other animals, bats have evolved to fill specialized niches, and these are often related to food types. Fruit bats, for instance, vary considerably in size. Small fruit bats specialize in locating and eating small fruits, such as figs, whereas large species can deal with much bigger fruits.

A similar relationship between body size and prey occurs in the insectivorous microbats, too. The insects that they seek are many and varied. The smallest species are not able to cope with catching big beetles, but some bigger bats actively seek them out. Insectivorous bats need to eat large numbers of insects each night. A pipistrelle, for instance, can increase its weight from 5 g (0.18 oz) to 7 g (0.25 oz) in just a few hours of feeding. These bats seek insects in places where they build up in large swarms such as in sheltered gardens, at lake or river sides and at forest edges.

SPECIAL DIETS

There are also specialists among the insect feeders. Long-eared bats, *Plecotus* sp., use their huge ears to hear the rustle of a moth in flight or an insect moving on a leaf. The Egyptian slit-faced bat, *Nycteris thebaica*, is adapted to catch scorpions on the ground, whereas the golden-tipped (or dome-headed) bat, *Kerivoula papuensi*, in Australia focuses on spiders that it snatches from their webs.

The slit-faced and golden-tipped bats are by no means the only microbats that take food other than insects. Some of the others have evolved to prey on many other food types from mammals, fish and blood to fruit, nectar and pollen, as described in the accounts of different microbat families (pp.55–107).

REDUCING COMPETITION

Such a varied selection of food types reduces the competition between species, so that many species can live in close proximity. As with most mammals, the availability of food affects population sizes. In the case of insectivorous bats, a major factor affecting insect numbers is the weather.

FINDING FOOD

Insect-eating bats are adapted to the short life-cycles of different insects. They soon learn where the insect swarms are at different times of the year and will fly many kilometres to feed on them. Noctules, *Nyctalus noctula*, in Britain for instance, have been known to suddenly start feeding at refuse dumps during the short period when crickets begin to emerge and fly. Insects are attracted to bright lights, such as street lights and illuminating stadiums, and bats soon arrive to feed.

Fruit bats always have to find new food supplies, as fruits on one tree do not last long with other fruit-eating animals around and fruiting trees may be scattered over a considerable area (see also p.47). The new feeding opportunity offered by a tree coming into fruit may be 10 km (6 miles) away from where the bats were feeding the night before.

Protecting a rich supply of food is usually done subtly by bats. Some microbats give out special shouts as they patrol up and down their feeding beat, and these may be warnings to others to stay away.

MOVEMENTS

Recent advances in technology have enabled researchers to attach radio transmitters to the backs of bats and track how far they fly. It is not unusual for small insectivorous bats such as pipistrelles to fly 2–3 km (1.2–1.8 miles) from their roost to feeding areas each night, and then spend several hours or more flying around feeding before returning to their roost. Some vesper bats, such as species of *Nyctalus* and *Myotis*, have been tracked moving more than 10 km (6 miles) on a regular basis. Various other species have been tracked flying up to 80 km (48 miles) each night and some, such as the free-tailed bats of the family Molossidae, even cross open water, as when they travel from an island to the mainland. Old World fruit bats, too, may regularly travel more than 50 km (30 miles) to a feeding area each night. Some bats move in this way for reasons other than feeding, such as roost-finding or socializing, although in many cases their motives are still unclear.

OPPOSITE This black flying fox, *Pteropus alecto*, from northern Australia and New Guinea has found an easy source of food. Unfortunately such habits can cause conflicts with commercial fruit growers and also New Guinean villages relying on their gardens for daily food.

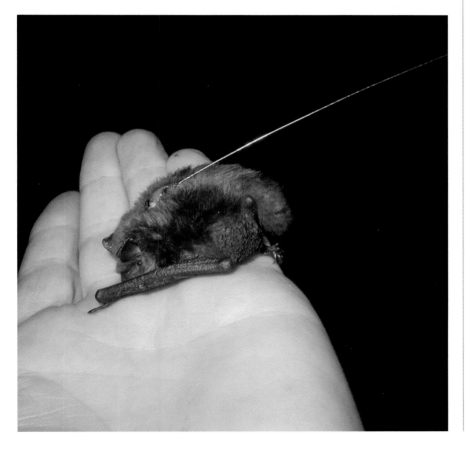

LEFT A bat fitted with a radio transmitter. These emit signals that can be detected up to a mile away.

ABOVE A metal clip fitted to the forearm of a juvenile Daubenton's bat, *Myotis daubentonii*. The unique number on the band enables researchers to track this individual's progress.

BAT-BANDING

Marking bats with lightweight metal bands on their forearms has enabled researchers to discover some details of their long-distance movements, and a number of patterns have been discovered. Bats in temperate areas travel from summer to winter hibernation sites, regularly over 20 km (12 miles) and sometimes over hundreds of kilometres. Some species, such as the noctule, *Nyctalus noctula*, and Nathusius' pipistrelle, *Pipistrellus nathusii*, move away from the cold north of Europe in autumn to the warmer south and west, and movements of over 1,000 km (600 miles) have been recorded. The hoary bat, *Lasiurus cinereus*, moves south for winter from Canada and northern USA, and probably reaches Mexico. This is yet another area where a great deal more information needs to be gathered, once technology has moved forward enough to help.

HOW BATS MAY NAVIGATE

It is still unclear how bats navigate over large distances. Certainly, echolocation has too short a range for high-flying bats, although lower down it may have a role. One sense that must be involved is vision. Bats remember how to travel a few kilometres

LEFT A whiskered bat, *Myotis mystacinus*, relies on echolocation when hunting for flying insects near the ground, but uses other senses including sight to navigate across landscapes.

each night to their feeding areas by following visually recognizable features, such as hedgerows, tall trees and roads. Perhaps navigation over greater distances involves other adaptations, such as an ability to detect magnetic variations or to orientate visually by the stars, or by sound or smell (each place may have a unique cocktail of odours for those species with the ability to detect them).

CHAPTER 3
Megabats

ANY OF THE MEGABATS OF THE FAMILY Pteropidae are called flying foxes because they have long dog-like muzzles, and some are known as blossom bats because they feed on nectar and pollen. These bats are found mostly in the tropics and subtropics, from Africa eastwards right across to Australia and the Pacific Islands. They have large eyes to enable them to navigate at night and this makes them look more attractive to humans than typical microbats.

With over 180 species, there is much variety in size and appearance. The largest include the large flying fox, *Pteropus vampyrus*, with a 1.7 m (5 ft 7 in) wingspan and the greater flying fox, *Pteropus neohibernicus*, with a weight of 1.5 kg (3.3 lb). The smallest include the spotted-winged fruit bat, *Baleonycteris maculata*, with a wingspan of less than 30 cm (12 in) and a weight of just 10 g (0.3 oz), the same as twenty paperclips.

The megabats, or Old World fruit bats, can be distinguished from the microbats by a number of distinctive features:

- long snout;
- wrap-around wings when hanging from perch;
- big eyes;
- second claw on finger as well as on thumb;
- lack of sophisticated echolocation system (primitive version only in some species);
- found throughout the tropical and subtropical regions from Africa and Asia to Australia; particularly diverse in Southeast Asia, New Guinea, Australia and some Pacific islands; absent from the Americas.

FOOD AND FEEDING

The bigger species of megabats take fruits and flowers from the canopy of trees, whereas the smaller species may feed lower down on smaller fruits. Their diet is sometimes supplemented with leaves and insects. The fruits taken, cover a

OPPOSITE A flying fox, *Pteropus* sp., with a long muzzle and large eyes for night navigation, roosting in a tree.

The northern blossom bat, *Macroglossus minimus*, is a small megabat with a 4 cm (1.6 in) forearm. The diet is mainly nectar and pollen. Males have a V-shaped scent gland on the upper chest, just visible in this picture, which it uses in communicating with others of its kind.

cross-section of all those available in a tropical habitat. The bats often land with outstretched wings on the treetops in order to pick off fruit. They take the fruits into their mouths and crush them between their teeth, tongue and hard palate. They swallow only the juice and soft part of the fruit, spitting out most of the skin and stones or seeds. Some bats eat the fruits while at the tree, but others may carry them off in their mouths to eat elsewhere.

There is a group of smaller megabats, placed in the sub-family Macroglossinae, that are nectar drinkers. They have evolved the ability to hover or land in front of flowers and stick their long tongues deep inside to drink the nectar, and they also eat the pollen. The Macroglossinae include the smallest fruit bats. Some have a little brush-like structure on the end of their tongues to help in collecting pollen and nectar.

FINDING ENOUGH FRUIT

Being governed by the seasons of spring, summer, autumn and winter, trees and shrubs in temperate regions tend to flower and fruit in a particular area at roughly the same time. Free from these seasonal influences, tropical forest trees and shrubs often reproduce at apparently random times (although wet and dry seasons in the tropics may complicate the picture). Also, whereas in temperate regions large numbers of relatively few tree species are concentrated in a particular area, in the

LEFT A flying fox, *Pteropus* sp., supported in this case by a diet of mango.

tropics far fewer individuals of many different species are scattered over a wide area. Fruit bats in the tropics, therefore, often have to search for a fruiting tree among tens of thousands of others that are not fruiting. This is where their keen sense of smell comes into play.

Another potential problem facing the fruit bats is that there is always plenty of competition from a great range of other animals such as monkeys, birds and insects, so a crop of fruit will not last long. All day and all night, the bats' rivals are busy eating the fruit. Those species that feed on flowers rather than fruit may have some advantages, because some flowers only open at night and emit scent solely to attract bats. The advantage to the flower is that it is pollinated in the process (see p.53).

MEGABAT ROOSTS

Typically, megabats roost out in the open, hanging communally from the upper branches of trees within a small area. They will use the same area for a time and then may set up camp in a new area, often following crops coming into fruit elsewhere.

BELOW Leschenault's rousettes, *Rousettus leschenaultia*, roosting in a Hong Kong tunnel, where they can echolocate with simple tongue-clicks. Unlike microbats, megabats like these have eye-shine, reflecting the photographer's flash.

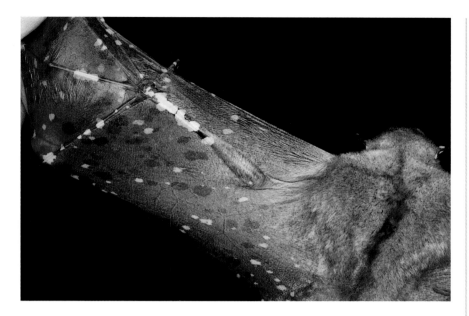

LEFT The cryptic markings on the bare parts of the Solomons tube-nosed fruit bat, *Nyctimene bougainville*, help camouflage this tree-roosting species when its wings are wrapped around its body.

Large camps may form, such as assemblies of as many as a million little red flying foxes, *Pteropus scapulatus*, in Australia, and may contain more than one species. These may remain in one site and become locally famous, or infamous in the case of huge roosts as the accumulated bat droppings from fruit bats create an overpowering smell.

BELOW Egyptian fruit bats, *Rousettus aegyptiacus*, roost in caves and even pyramids. They are depicted on tomb artwork thousands of years old.

Some fruit bats, on the other hand, roost in small numbers, while others, such as the epauletted fruit bats, *Epomops*, of Africa, sleep alone. Some camps are set up in mangroves and above marshes, possibly for protection from predators, although megabats always seem to be relatively active throughout the day as well as the night, so any approach by a predator would be likely to disturb them and cause them to fly. Tube-nosed fruit bats, *Nyctimene* sp., have another method of protection, being camouflaged with yellow spots on their wings and ears so that they look like curled-up leaves when roosting.

Some species of fruit bats, such as some of the bare-backed fruit bats, *Dobsonia* sp., some of the nectar-feeding bats like *Eonycteris* sp., and the rousette fruit bats, *Rousettus* sp., roost in caves. Roosting places are often just inside the cave where there is some light, but *Rousettus* can penetrate into the darker depths as it can echolocate by tongue-clicking and listening for the echo, so producing a cruder version of the microbats' echolocation system.

BIZARRE MEGABATS

Although they generally look more appealing to most people than many of the microbats, some Old World fruit bats have strange features. The tube-nosed fruit bats, *Nyctimene* sp., have tubular nostrils that extend outwards from the face at an angle of about 45° and the reason for this is unknown. The nostrils have been observed moving as the bats produce calls, so there may be some form of echolocation involved, but these creatures have been little studied. It may be more likely that the nostrils help give the bats a more exact determination of the position of fruits by allowing them to smell in 'stereo'. They feed in the very dark conditions under the canopy in forests so a greater directionality to their sense of smell would be beneficial.

Another megabat with a very strange appearance is the African hammer-headed fruit bat, *Hypsignathus monstrosus*, in which the males have a greatly enlarged, rectangular muzzle rather like the head of a hammer, as well as huge pendulous lips, a warty snout and ruffles of skin around the mouth. The hammer shape is associated with the amazingly loud sounds made by the males to attract females (see pp.34–35). The bare-backed fruit bats, *Dobsonia* sp., are also odd-looking. They have a membrane of skin across their backs joining the flight membrane of their wings, which accounts for their name. This unusual feature of these cave-roosting bats brings them some advantage linked to flight and foraging.

ABOVE A Solomons tube-nosed fruit bat, *Nyctimene bougainville*, showing its large eyes for good vision in dark conditions, and its extended nostrils.

ISLAND ISOLATION

Megabats have colonized many islands in the Indian and Pacific Oceans. The more isolated islands may have been colonized by accident, by typhoon-swept bats or bats blown off course that kept on flying until they reached land. Once they arrived, those that survived began to fit into an environment that was different from their original homeland. Ensuing generations changed and became more in tune with their new surroundings. Eventually, new species developed.

There are today a number of islands with small populations of endemic fruit bats. If a natural disaster such as a typhoon were to strike, the entire species might be decimated or even wiped out altogether. Humans are also increasingly making their mark and rapidly modifying the landscape with mining, deforestation, farming and house-building. The bats cannot adapt sufficiently quickly to the changed conditions, so there are serious risks of extinctions on these islands.

As if these threats were not enough, protein sources are often scarce and people living on the islands have relied for centuries on fruit bats to supplement their diet. This used to be a sustainable harvest, but nowadays the increasing human populations are literally eating into the bat populations. On the western Pacific island of Guam, large numbers of bats from other places are even imported as food, because those on the island have already been hunted to extinction.

CONFLICT

In many countries, such as Australia, South Africa and Israel, commercial fruit growing is an important industry. When the local fruit bats see hectares of fruiting trees they are naturally attracted and descend, sometimes in their thousands, to feed. Fruit growers have tried scaring them away by such methods as detonating exploding devices, shooting the bats, driving them away from their nearby day roosts and erecting nets around the crop.

In Israel, during the 1950s and 1960s, many caves with roosting bats were fumigated in a mistaken belief that these held fruit bats, resulting in the deaths of many thousands of innocent insect-eating bats. All this persecution might be largely unnecessary anyway as the bats are more attracted to ripe fruit, which they can locate at night by smell and which are softer to eat. It is often the unripe fruit that is picked by the growers and allowed to ripen on its way to the consumers, or sold slightly unripe so that it will be ripe when needed. Despite this, the unfortunate fruit bats are usually portrayed as the villains.

Large camps of fruit bats can be noisy and smelly, and when the bats gather in force in urban areas this can cause serious local protest, especially if they are a million strong. In Australia, a number of such conflicts have been resolved by education initiatives in the local community, informing people how essential fruit bats are in pollinating flowers.

The plight of island fruit bats, and the problems this can bring for the human population, can be highlighted by the example of the Solomon Islands in the South Pacific, an area that has at least 11 endemic species of fruit bats, some living only on single islands. Large amounts of timber are currently being extracted and exported from these islands. As the forests are felled, the bats are losing both their roosting places and food supplies. One or two of the smaller islands have been completely cleared of their forest cover and now the locals are beginning to realize the terrible effect deforestation has on their land, the soil is being washed away and they are struggling to grow crops.

The Bougainville monkey-faced bat, *Pteralopex anceps*, was thought to have become extinct, but a single specimen was found on the island of Choiseul in the Solomons in the late 1990s by a university expedition from Britain. Unfortunately, huge areas of forest on Choiseul have already been sold off to timber merchants, who have already begun to clear them. Although the local people are now beginning to have second thoughts, it may be too late. Having cleared forest along the coast, the loggers are now working their way up to the high central ridge where this rare bat lives, and its future looks bleak. Much of the timber obtained is used to make a decidedly non-essential product, barbecue charcoal.

SURVIVING EXTINCTION

On the Indian Ocean island whose name they bear, Rodrigues flying foxes were all but extinct due to deforestation until some of the last individuals were taken into captivity and bred in a few specialist zoos in Britain and the USA. Numbers in captivity are now increasing, and it is hoped to release some back into the wild in places where some of the original habitat still exists; but not on Rodrigues, where the habitat has been destroyed, but on other islands in the area.

A VITAL RELATIONSHIP

OPPOSITE Hanging by a thread, the nearly extinct Rodrigues flying fox, *Pteropus rodricensis*, looks out on a grim future.

When fruit bats eat fruits they are helping the tree from which they are feeding. The bats spit out most of the seeds or stones and some of these then germinate where they land and grow into new trees. Although some bats dine at the tree, others will take the fruit some distance and so disperse the seeds over a large area. Some of the seeds are swallowed and these quickly go through the bats' digestive systems and are deposited later, often far away from the parent tree, in the animals' droppings. These then act as convenient packages of fertilizer for the seedlings that develop. Bats that feed on nectar and pollen inadvertently accumulate pollen on their fur and so pollinate other flowers when they move around the forest.

In a beautiful process of co-evolution, some plants have evolved in intimate partnership with certain bat species so that they can be of mutual benefit. The flower has evolved to be attractive only to bats in various ways. For instance, its shape may be just right for the muzzle and tongue of the bat to fit into it and obtain the nectar and pollen, or the flower may open and produce scent only at night. The male parts of the flower are adapted so that some of the pollen is transferred to the fur of the feeding bat, in precisely the right place for it to fertilize another flower when the bat moves on to another plant of the same species.

A good example of a bat-pollinated tree is the durian, *Durio zibethinus*, of Southeast Asia, whose remarkably pungent-smelling fruits are regarded as a great delicacy in the region, where they are of considerable commercial importance. The durian's flowers open at dusk and are visited and pollinated by flying foxes. The baobab tree, *Adansonia digitata*, of Africa is another example of a species with bat-pollinated flowers. In all such cases, if the bats are destroyed, there will be no pollination, and hence none of the trees that rely on them. As well as maintaining an existing supply of trees, bats are a vital part of tropical forest regeneration. Volcanic islands emerging in the middle of an ocean have been partly vegetated as a result of visiting fruit bats depositing their seed-containing guano.

CHAPTER 4

Microbats I

WITH 17 FAMILIES AND MORE than 900 species, the mostly insectivorous microbats are far more diverse than the fruit-eating megabats. They are not restricted to tropical areas, as insects can be found almost everywhere, and so the microbats are found in all terrestrial areas of the world except in the coldest regions. They are generally smaller than the Old World fruit bats, although there is much overlap in size. The biggest microbats have a huge wingspan of almost a metre (3 ft) and weigh almost 200 g (7 oz). The smallest microbat is a tiny creature, with a wingspan of about 15 cm (6 in) and a weight of only 1.7–2 g (0.06–0.07 oz).

WEIRD FACES

The faces of some species of microbat are bizarre-looking. Microbats rely heavily on their echolocation system at night and this has developed in different ways for different species. Many have developed odd-looking noses, with a leaf-like arrangement of skin to help with sound emission, while others use their mouths for the same purpose. Some have large pimple-like scent glands on their snouts to enable them to communicate with other bats using smell. Many microbats also have odd-shaped ears to collect the quiet echoes that bounce back from their targets. In addition, some bats have folds of skin on their faces, the purpose of which has yet to be discovered. The wrinkle-faced bat, *Centurio senex*, for instance, which is found from Mexico to Venezuela and Trinidad, has a large amount of loose skin that folds down over its face when it hangs itself up in its roost.

Microbats are easily recognized by the following features, which distinguish them from the macrobats (see p.45):
- they usually have short snouts;
- they usually have small eyes;
- they usually fold their wings alongside their bodies;
- they often have strange-looking noses and large ears, which aid in echolocation.

ABOVE The barbastelle, *Barbastella barbastellus*, a member of the family Vespertilionidae, sometimes echolocates through its mouth, sometimes through its nose.

OPPOSITE A striped hairy-nosed bat, *Mimon crenulatum*, feeding on a katydid. This is one of the great New World family of bats, the Phyllostomidae, with a very large, spear-shaped nose-leaf. Microbats such as this with very large ears often use them to listen for the sounds of their insect prey.

MICROBAT DIETS

Insectivorous bats have spread out to fill every available insect-feeding niche. The aerial hawkers are the most common, but others glean insects from leaves or the ground. Some specialize in catching spiders rather than insects. It was not too big a leap of evolution for some of these bats to become carnivores and start feeding on amphibians, birds and small mammals, including other bats.

When they colonized the Americas, early microbats found a huge selection of fruit available in the tropical forests but no fruit bats, so some of them evolved to become fruit-eaters. Other microbats developed the habit of feeding on nectar and pollen, so filling that niche too in the same way as the megabats had already done in the Old World. They have the advantage that some can switch to insects, and regularly feed on both plant and animal matter.

Then there are the oddities, those microbat species that have a different diet and lifestyle from the majority. A number of species have become specialized for catching fish, snatching them from the water using their large strong feet equipped with big hooked claws. Most famous, or infamous, are the three small species of vampire bats, all in Central and South America, that feed exclusively on the fresh blood of mammals and birds. Although thinking about this may send a shiver down some people's spines, this is exactly what mosquitoes do each time they bite you. To obtain their blood meals, vampire bats usually seek out horses, cattle, chickens and other domestic animals, or any other sleeping mammals or birds that they can climb onto, but they do not often drink human blood.

NOCTILIONIDAE The two species in this family are the fisherman bats of Central and South America, also called bulldog bats from their appearance. The larger of the two, *Noctilio leporinus*, has evolved to fish for most of its food in freshwater ponds, lakes and rivers and inshore waters of the sea. It uses echolocation to detect ripples on the surface of still water, then gaffs fish up to 7 cm (2.75 in) long with the long, hooked claws on the toes of its huge feet. The bat then flies off, carrying its prey, to a perch, hangs up and eats its catch. It also uses its feet to catch insects. The smaller species, *Noctilio albiventris*, is strictly an insect-eater, a fisherman bat that doesn't fish. It takes most of its insects from the water surface.

CRASEONYCTERIDAE The single species Kitti's hog-nosed bat, *Craseonycteris thonglongyai*, sometimes called the bumblebee or butterfly bat, is found only in a few caves along the border between Thailand and Myanmar (Burma). Not discovered until 1973 by the Thai mammal researcher Dr Kitti Thonglongya (for whom it was named) this is the smallest bat in the world and possibly the smallest mammal, too (an African shrew competes for this title). It has a forearm only 2.5 cm (1 in) long and weighs about 2 g (0.07 oz) or less. In the depths of its cave roosts it has been seen flying with great agility in and out of tunnels no larger than a fox's burrow. Outside, this tiny bat forages for insects around teak forest and bamboo clumps.

ANALYZING DIETS

Insect-eating bats may carry individual large insects off to a perch and devour them there at their leisure, or may feed on many hundreds of insects each night, eating them as they fly. It has been estimated that the huge roosts of free-tailed bats in Texas eat about 10,000 tonnes (9,850 tons) of insects each year. The types of insects taken can be identified and their relative numbers ascertained from the microscopic analysis of the bats' droppings. Such analysis from archaeological sites

MYSTACINIDAE Today, this New Zealand family contains just a single species, the lesser short-tailed bat, *Mystacina tuberculata* (its very close relative the greater short-tailed bat, *Mystacina robusta*, is now thought to be extinct). This remarkable bat evolved to feed on the ground and can fold each wing into a leathery pouch alongside its body so that it can run around looking for insects without damaging its wings. It also catches large numbers of insects in flight. The lesser short-tailed bat also eats pollen and fruit during part of the year, and there is evidence that it is a major pollinator of some plants. Its sturdy legs, feet and very sharp claws are adapted for running on the ground and climbing trees, just like a rodent. The fur is thick and similar to that of a shrew (family Soricidae). Some of the tree cavities in which it has been found roosting show signs of being enlarged by the bats chewing at the wood.

THYROPTERIDAE The three species in this Central and South American family, all in the genus *Thyroptera*, are known as disc-winged bats. The discs are suckers on the thumb and soles of the feet that help the bat to maintain a firm grip when roosting on the underside of shiny leaves, such as banana leaves. The Old World sucker-footed bat, *Myzopoda aurita*, of Madagascar, the single member of the family Myzopodidae, has almost identical suckers to the three *Thyroptera* species. Although they live thousands of miles apart on different continents, the two groups of bats have evolved precisely the same adaptation. It is possible that they are close relatives that became isolated in the very distant past, but on the other hand they may be an excellent example of convergent evolution in which unrelated organisms evolve similar adaptations for a similar lifestyle.

OPPOSITE LEFT The lesser bulldog bat, *Noctilio albiventris*, uses its large feet to snatch insects from the surface of water.

OPPOSITE RIGHT Kitti's hog-nosed bat, *Craseonycteris thonglongyai*, the world's smallest mammal, is classed as endangered.

LEFT These Spix's disc-winged bats, *Thyroptera tricolor*, are roosting by gripping the inside of a *Heliconia* leaf with the suction pads on their thumbs and feet.

has shown that the composition of plant species in ancient landscapes, as identified from the pollen on the insect fragments, is very different from that determined by looking at the pollen in peat layers in bogs. The latter involves plants that are mainly wind-pollinated, whereas the former involves insect-pollinated plants. Such studies of bat droppings are changing scientists' ideas about the make-up of ancient landscapes. Insect analysis from droppings also tells us how the diet of a species changes during the year as different insects become available.

MICROBAT ROOSTS

Unlike megabats, the great majority of microbats tend to roost well out of sight, deep inside a building, tree or cave. Some species, such as the red bat, *Lasiurus borealis*, of North America and the tent-building bats, *Uroderma*, *Artibeus* and *Ectophylla* spp. (see p.83) do roost in the open, but these exceptions to the rule tend to be few in number, very quiet and well-camouflaged and usually remain sheltered beneath leaves.

Many species of microbats roost in tree crevices. They enter holes in the trunk or branches made and then abandoned by woodpeckers or resulting from rot, insect or storm damage, preferring to roost deep inside the tree where the centre has rotted away. Others roost beneath loose bark or between climbing plants and the trunk. Many microbats use caves. Different species penetrate and roost at different distances from the entrance, depending on their precise needs for temperature and humidity levels.

Many species have benefited from the advent of humans and the structures they have conveniently scattered around the landscape. House roofs and walls are commonly used as roost sites, different species of bats preferring different designs. For instance, the long-eared bat, *Plecotus auritus*, in Britain prefers to roost in large open loft spaces, whereas the pipistrelle, *Pipistrellus pipistrellus*, is happier tucked into the tiny space of the boxed-in eaves at the roof edge. Bats roost behind shutters,

BELOW A group of serotines, *Eptesicus serotinus*, roost against the ridge beam in a house roof-space.

hanging tiles, weatherboarding, anything that gives them a bit of protection. Churches, large mansions, old stone or brick stable blocks, and hospitals are also popular roost sites. Bats make ample use of the diversity of structures that humans have erected, from towers to tunnels, and from bridges to basements.

ABOVE Mexican free-tailed bats, *Tadarida brasiliensis*, emerge from Congress Avenue Bridge in Austin, Texas, USA to great acclaim.

All these roosts have common features, they provide the bats with a dark place where they can hang up high and safe where no predator can reach them. Often the entrance is small and narrow, just allowing the bats to squeeze through. When necessary, they can immediately take flight simply by dropping from their perch.

Many typical roosts contain only a single species of bat, but bigger ones may contain several species, roosting in separate places within the site. Numbers vary with the species involved and what the bats are doing. Many species form all-female roosts when producing young. The greatest numbers occur when the females are in maternity roosts, which can contain anything from tens of individuals to vast numbers. For instance, about 1.5 million Mexican free-tailed bats, *Tadarida brasiliensis*, roost each summer under the Congress Avenue Bridge in Austin, Texas, in the heart of an urban environment, whereas much smaller roosts of about 40 or fewer long-eared bats, *Plecotus auritus*, are found in buildings in Europe.

Microbats use their roosts for a great variety of purposes as well as for sleeping. These include mating, giving birth and caring for young, gathering in spring and autumn, keeping cool, keeping warm, socializing and digesting food.

HIBERNATION AND HIBERNACULA

In areas of the world where winter temperatures are low, insect-eating bats are unable to find enough food to stay active. Migrating to warmer climates is a possibility and some species do this (see pp.41–42, 103), but many hibernate instead.

Hibernation is a state similar to a very deep sleep where the whole metabolism slows down. The bat allows its body temperature to fall almost to that of the environment; the colder it is, the slower the bat's metabolism. The heartbeat falls to about 20 beats a minute and breathing can slow to only five breaths a minute and becomes very irregular.

Hibernating bats can even survive freezing conditions for short periods, but usually choose shelters with temperatures of about 5°C (41°F). They keep their bodies just surviving in this way by slowly burning the fat that they stored within them during the autumn. They are unusual in this respect, being members of a select band of vertebrates called heterotherms, which can maintain their own body temperature, but are also able to allow it to drop, as happens in hibernation. By contrast, most other mammals, including humans, are homoiotherms, they maintain a fairly stable body temperature, requiring a steady supply of energy throughout the year. Some

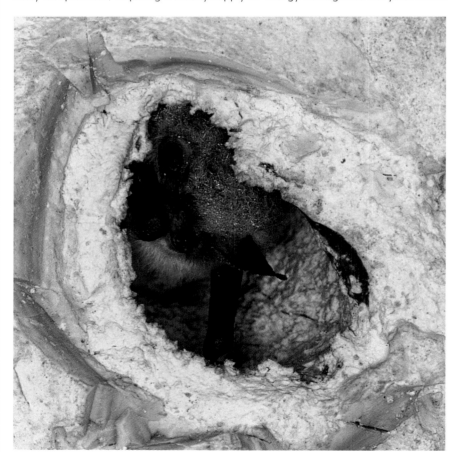

RIGHT A Natterer's bat, *Myotis nattereri*, hibernating in a natural crevice only 3 cm (1.2 in) across in a cave roof.

TORPOR

In temperate regions in summer the weather may be cold and wet for many days, resulting in few insects flying for the bats to feed on. Homoiotherms, such as humans, lose more body heat at such times so have to increase their energy intake. Bats cannot do this as their food is not available, but they are able to become torpid and so use little energy. The condition of torpor may last for days until conditions improve and enough insects are flying again. Some torpid bats have been recorded surviving without food or water for as long as two weeks on end.

Torpor is similar to hibernation, but usually occurs at warmer temperatures and for a shorter time, and bats can drop into this state at any time of the year. Again, as during hibernation, they allow their body temperature to fall almost to that of the environment. Bats will select specific roost sites that are cold so that they can become torpid and survive lean periods, then move back into warmer sites once the weather has improved. Night roosts may be cold places. Having fed, the bats can spend the rest of the hours of darkness in a night roost and use up little energy by becoming torpid. For pregnant bats, however, going torpid slows the development inside the womb, another factor in the complex balance between energy needs and choice of roost site.

Interestingly, a whole cluster of bats may go torpid, but how this communal decision is made or which bat decides when to wake up and warm up, which will warm up the whole cluster, is not yet understood.

other creatures, such as reptiles, are ectotherms, they have relatively low metabolic rates and their body temperatures are affected directly by the temperature of the environment. Snakes and butterflies bask in the sun, absorbing energy so that they can warm up and become active. If it becomes too hot, they seek shade, moving around to different sites to maintain their best working temperature. When it is cold their metabolisms slow right down and they need very little energy to stay alive.

Hibernation is not a continuous process. A group of hibernating bats will arouse themselves after a few days or weeks or a month. At such times they may feed, given the opportunity. They will also move sites, if necessary, to select one more suitable for their condition, for instance, a colder roost will slow down their metabolism. Triggers that may cause bats to arouse include slight changes in temperature, disturbance from noise, lights or touch, the time of day or year and the need to drink or urinate. It takes up to an hour for them to increase their metabolism enough to fly.

CHOOSING THE RIGHT SITE

The hibernaculum needs to be a place where the bats can cool down to just the right temperature so that they will use little energy over winter. It must also be humid so that the bats do not become dehydrated. As with roost sites, different species prefer different conditions, so a large hibernaculum may contain many species, but all at slightly different temperatures in different places within the site. The hibernaculum must also maintain a fairly stable set of conditions, even if the temperature outside changes, otherwise the bats may wake as they warm up or cool down. Waking up wastes valuable stored energy, so bats try to limit the number of times this occurs. The places offering all these conditions tend to be underground sites, such as caves, mines, bunkers, cellars, ice-houses and tunnels. The temperature at the entrance is close to that outside, but deeper within the site conditions are buffered.

ABOVE This whiskered bat, *Myotis mystacinus*, hibernating in a mine is covered in silvery drops of condensation.

Bats may hibernate in large numbers, and some east European caves hold tens of thousands of bats each winter. Although the bats may cluster together, it is just as common to see bats singly. Trying to count the number of bats is difficult. They are not moving and may be tucked deep into a crevice with perhaps just a nose poking out here and there. Many individuals may be visible only from certain angles, though some species, such as horseshoe bats, hang exposed from the roof. Condensation may form on the fur, making a bat look unnaturally pale or even white, so species identification can be problematical. The numbers of individuals hibernating increase during the winter, with maximum numbers in the last half of winter, when conditions are usually most severe.

CARNIVOROUS BATS

Some of the insect-eating microbats have evolved a different diet, and eat larger prey as well. Here we take a look at two of the families involved, although not all of the members of these families are carnivorous.

SLIT-FACED BATS

The slit-faced bats that make up the family Nycteridae, all placed in the genus *Nycteris*, consist of some 16 species that live in Africa and Asia, as far east as Java. The common name refers to the deep groove that extends along the length of the muzzle and forehead, ending in the nostrils. A fleshy nose-leaf and fur cover this slit to some extent, but they are strange-looking bats with big ears. Most eat insects and spiders, which they hunt in a variety of mainly drier habitats from semi-deserts to woodland savannah. The Egyptian slit-faced bat, *Nycteris thebaica*, is a scorpion specialist, which alights on the ground to find prey, its large ears enabling it to hear the quietest of movements.

THE RHYTHM OF LIFE

All mammals have a circadian rhythm, an inbuilt system that tells them when day and night occur, even in the darkness of a cave. We humans have it too, and notice it on long-haul airplane flights when we cross time zones, we call it 'jet-lag'. Bats can tell precisely when it is time to emerge from their roosts, even in temperate zones where the day-lengths change. They are able to sense seasons, too, and have a similar internal 'clock' that tells them when to shut down and hibernate for winter and when to arouse because spring has arrived. This is triggered by changes in day-length as well as temperature changes.

Slit-faced bats roost in small numbers in the usual kinds of roost sites, trees, wells, caves and buildings. Some have even been found down the burrows of aardvarks. The most voracious predator in the family is the biggest, the large slit-faced bat, *Nycteris grandis*. Even then it is no giant, with a forearm length of only 6 cm (2.4 in). It eats just about anything that moves and that it can get its teeth into such as frogs, birds, other bats and fish. The prey are usually on the small side and not likely to fight back too fiercely. This species can be found across the central part of Africa and down the eastern side.

ABOVE The hairy slit-faced bat, *Nycteris hispida*, is a common bat throughout much of southern Africa, often roosting alone in rooms in disused buildings.

LEFT Dobson's slit-faced bat, *Nycteris macrotis*, seen here in a hollow tree, lives in equatorial African moist woodland and often roosts solitarily.

RIGHT Yellow-winged bats, *Lavia frons*, this is the only species in the family Megadermatidae that is not a carnivore.

FALSE VAMPIRES

The false vampire bats (Megadermatidae) make up a smaller family of five species. They were originally thought to drink blood, hence their common name, but this proved not to be true. Four of the five species are carnivores, with a wide diet that includes small birds, mammals including other bats and mice, reptiles and large numbers of insects. The fifth member of the family, the yellow-winged bat, *Lavia frons*, feeds only on insects.

All members of this family are spectacular and distinctive, with large eyes (for microbats), huge upright ears and a big upright nose leaf. Two species live in Africa: the African false vampire bat, *Cardioderma cor*, occurs in northeast Africa, from Eritrea south to central Tanzania, and the yellow-winged bat, *Lavia frons*, is found across a broad belt of central Africa, from Gambia east to Ethiopia and south to northern Zambia. There are also two species in Asia, the greater false vampire bat, *Megaderma lyra*, and lesser false vampire bats, *Megaderma spasma*, are found from Afghanistan south through India to Sri Lanka and east as far as China and the Philippines. The Australian false vampire bat, *Macroderma gigas*, usually known as the ghost bat, is found only in the tropical north of Australia.

HUNTING PREY

With their large eyes, it is likely that the false vampires hunt visually to some extent, but they also use their big ears to detect the slightest rustling of their prey on the ground. Typically, a false vampire hangs from a perch in a tree and watches and listens for small animals, flying down and pouncing as soon as it has detected suitably prey. After a while, it moves on and tries its luck from another tree. Sometimes, the bat will cruise along low over the ground, looking and listening for prey. Although it can also use echolocation to pinpoint its target, the sounds it emits are very quiet, merely a whisper, so as not to alarm the potential prey.

When catching a rodent, a false vampire drops down on it and covers it with its wings, then delivers the *coup de grâce* by a bite to the victim's neck. Larger prey are taken back to the roost to eat. These bats do not seem to travel very far each night and radio-tracking has shown that distances of only about 2 km (1.25 miles) are involved. In Australia some ghost bats prey upon a cave roost of 20,000 orange leaf-nosed bats, *Rhinonycteris aurantius*, nightly. The ghost bats fly up above the cave entrance and then zoom down to gain speed and hit the stream of emerging prey.

The ghost bat, *Macroderma gigas*, is one of the biggest microbats in the world, with a forearm length of about 11 cm (4.3 in) and a wingspan of approximately 70 cm (28 in). It is a very pale bat with whitish fur and skin. Like other false vampire bats, ghost bats may roost in small groups or in colonies up to 1,500 strong. They generally prefer to roost among rocks, and may be found among piles of boulders as well as in limestone caves and old mines.

The insectivorous African yellow-winged bat, *Lavia frons*, is unusual in often hunting during the daytime. It has an attractive dove-grey fur (sometimes yellow underneath), contrasting with striking bright orange-yellow flight membranes and ears.

BELOW The ghost bat, *Macroderma gigas*, of northern Australia commonly preys on house mice, *Mus musculus*.

THE ERUPTION OF TROUBLE AT MOUNT ETNA

The Mount Etna in question is not the famous volcano in Sicily, but a large limestone area near Rockhampton, in the state of Queensland, Australia, riddled with holes and caverns. Some of these housed ghost bats, *Macroderma gigas*, and some 100,000 bent-winged bats, *Miniopterus australis*, in what were spectacular cave systems loved by cavers.

During the 1960s, a large cement-making company started to quarry the limestone and the troubles started. Some of the area had been given reserve status, but the state withdrew this as the blasting and quarrying continued. The Queensland Premier declared the area with most bats a reserve again in 1988, but the cement company continued its destructive work. The national government declared its concern, but did not interfere. Pressure mounted from both Australian and international conservationists to stop the destruction. Meanwhile, the roosting areas were damaged in an attempt to destroy them before the quarrying reached them. The cement company stated that it was vital to extract the particular quality of limestone found near the roosting bats, so they continued with their plans and blew up one of the most important roosting sites for the ghost bats. They then proceeded to dump spoil from elsewhere down into some of the cavities without attempting any extraction of the rock. This is just one example where wildlife is given a back seat as big money and jobs take precedence.

The ghost bat used to live across most of Australia and was still recorded in central parts in 1960. This endemic species has declined dramatically and now is only found on the northern edges of the country. Accordingly, it has been classed as vulnerable by the International Union for Conservation of Nature (IUCN).

HORSESHOE AND OLD WORLD LEAF-NOSED BATS

Members of two microbat families have the most bizarre-looking noses imaginable, their structure having evolved to help them echolocate (see pp.23–27). Instead of 'shouting' out their bursts of ultrasound from their mouths, bats in these two families 'snort' the sounds out through their nostrils and have some very strangely shaped noses that may help them direct the sound. It is possible that some of these weird noses have other purposes, too.

HORSESHOE BATS

There are over 70 species in the family Rhinolophidae, commonly known as horseshoe bats, and they are distributed widely in the Old World, from the tropics to temperate regions, and from Ireland and Africa across Europe and southern Asia eastwards to Japan and Australia. The common name aptly describes the shape of part of the nose leaf. The nostrils are surrounded by a horseshoe-shaped area of thick skin that also covers the upper lip and has a small notch in it at the centre of the lip. This nose leaf continues and forms a free-standing flattened spike above the nostrils, called the lancet. Between the two is a third part to this complex skin structure, the sella. It is flattened from side to side so its edge sticks forwards and it has peculiar folds attaching it to the face. These three parts are of different shapes and sizes in different species and are commonly used by bat researchers to distinguish one species from another.

LEFT The greater horseshoe bat, *Rhinolophus ferrumequinum*, showing the three-part nose-leaf and lack of tragus. This species occurs from Britain right across Europe and Asia to as far east as Japan.

Many horseshoe bats are pale sandy or grey in colour, but there are black species and species with orange fur, as well as others that have two colour phases, some individuals being grey and some orange.

LARGE EARS AND FALSE NIPPLES

There are some other differences between this family and many other families of bats. Horseshoe bats have quite large ears that they can move independently, while many other bats have to move the whole head to change their hearing direction. Also the ear has no tragus sticking up within it. Interesting extras are a couple of nipple-like structures on the female, on either side of her abdomen, that are used by the youngsters to hang on to when they are moved by their mothers. Few other kinds of bats have these useful false teats.

Horseshoe bats are also unusual among the microbats in that they wrap their wings around themselves when resting, whereas most of the others fold them along their sides. In a neat example of packaging, the tail membrane is curled up to plug a small gap at the back that is not covered by the wings.

DISTINCTIVE ECHOLOCATION

With noses like theirs it is hardly surprising there are differences in the way horseshoe bats echolocate compared with many other microbat families. The snorts of ultrasound they emit are all at roughly the same frequency, whereas each of the shouts produced by other microbats sweeps down from a high to lower frequency (see p.23). The horseshoe bats' constant-frequency calls seem to be particularly good at providing lots of information about moving targets, especially the wing-beats of an insect.

HORSESHOE BAT LIFESTYLES

With so many species of horseshoe bats, there is great variety in their lifestyles, but generally they emerge late when it is quite dark and feed just on insects, although they sometimes eat spiders, too. They are able to land and take off from the ground (a number of other bats cannot do this) and part of their diet includes insects such as beetles snatched from the ground. Prey are taken to a roost and eaten, and indigestible parts, such as the body cases, legs and wings of insects, are discarded beneath, leaving a record of what the bat has been eating each night.

RIGHT Horseshoe bats, such as this greater horseshoe bat, *Rhinolophus ferrumequinum*, have short tails and tail membranes.

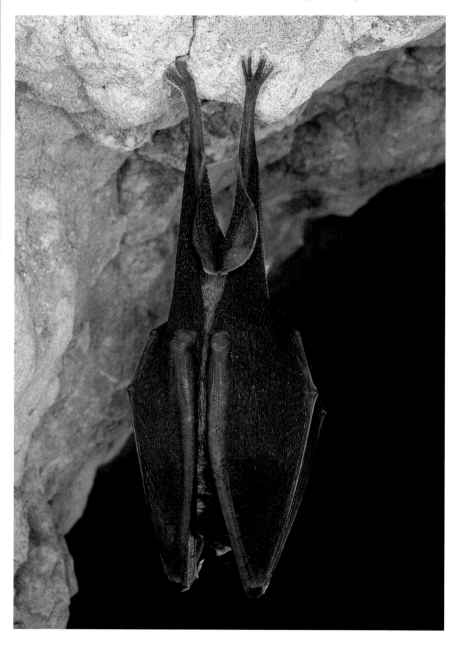

Each bat tends to have its own foraging areas and arrives there each night from the day roost using the same routes. Different species of horseshoe bats are adapted to life in a great range of habitats, from arid areas to wet woodlands. Those that live in colder climates hibernate in nearby caves or mines and hang in exposed clusters from the roof, not tucked into crevices like other bats. They tend to select the warmer hibernacula and do not go into such deep hibernation as other bat species in the area.

Roosting sites are the usual mixture of natural and man-made structures, but horseshoe bats tend to prefer sites they can fly straight into. They do not like stopping at an entrance, crawling through a narrow gap and then continuing deep into the roost, the preferred method for many other microbats. A barn roof, therefore, may be used if there is an open window leading straight into the attic.

ABOVE As with all bat species, these greater horseshoe bat babies, *Rhinolophus ferrumequinum,* are left hanging up in the nursery when their mothers leave to feed each night. This nursery is sited inside a house roof.

CHASTITY PLUG

An interesting aspect of the breeding behaviour of horseshoe bats, certainly in the greater horseshoe bat, *Rhinolophus ferrumequinum* (a species found right across the southern Palaearctic biogeographic region, from Britain to Japan), is that after mating in autumn the females develop a waxy plug in the vaginal opening that effectively prevents further matings. This plug forms from secretions from the male and hardens once inside the female. It is expelled as soon as the female ovulates and the egg is fertilized by her partner's stored sperm in spring. Collections of plugs found under roosting sites give some idea of pregnancy rates.

CATCHING INSECTS

Different techniques are used by different species in different situations.

GLEANING Some bat species, such as long-eared bats, *Plecotus*, can hover or fly very slowly and can detect, then take, insects from the surface of leaves.

FLY-CATCHING Some, like the horseshoe bats, *Rhinolophus*, and the yellow-winged bat, *Lavia frons* (one of the false vampire bats), may hang up from a perch in the feeding area and sally forth to catch an insect, then return to the perch.

IN FLIGHT Many take their flying insect prey while flying along. Some, such as pipistrelles, *Pipistrellus*, take large numbers of tiny insects from swarms straight into their mouths (stiff, touch-sensitive hairs around the mouths help here). Others, such as serotines, *Eptesicus*, take larger insects directly into the mouth or may catch them in the wing or tail membrane and bend their heads down to transfer them to their mouths. Some, like Daubenton's bat, *Myotis daubentonii*, use their feet to catch the insects, then reach down to transfer them to their mouths (the toes have touch-sensitive hairs). Some species take larger prey items back to a roost and devour them there, digest the food (when they are warm, bats can digest food very quickly), and then set off again to catch more.

POUNCING Some species, such as the horseshoe bats, *Rhinolophus*, fly close to the ground and, on detecting prey, pounce on it, surrounding it with their outstretched wings. They then reach underneath their bodies and grab their prey with the mouth.

LEFT Microbats often use a wing to scoop insects out of the air. Here, a greater horseshoe bat, *Rhinolophus ferrumequinum*, is about to catch a moth.

DIVERSITY OF SPECIES

The greater horseshoe bat, *Rhinolophus ferrumequinum*, is one of the bigger horseshoe bats, with a 6 cm (2.4 in) forearm and 40 cm (16 in) wingspan. The great woolly horseshoe bat, *Rhinolophus luctus*, found from India to Borneo, can have a forearm up to 7.5 cm (3 in) long, which makes it the biggest member of the family. The little Nepalese horseshoe bat, *Rhinolophus subbadius*, is the smallest, not much bigger than a pipistrelle with a forearm length of about 3 cm (1.2 in). The lesser horseshoe bat, *Rhinolophus hipposideros*, is only a little bigger. This species is found from Ireland to Central Asia.

Greater horseshoe bats, *Rhinolophus ferrumequinum*, in the UK have been well-studied for over a hundred years and have been known for far longer (for example, there is a record of Oliver Cromwell reporting this species in Corfe Castle in Dorset in 1650). In the late 1800s, they could be found all along the south of England, but now occur only in the southwest. Reasons for this drastic decline include changes in farming practices that have affected insect numbers. Hayfields are now relatively rare, for instance, and much grass is now cut early and turned into silage, so insect life cycles are also cut short. Recent studies have found that dosing cows with chemicals to control intestinal worms also kills all the beetles, which feed on the cow pats that appear afterwards in the fields. These insects are an important part of the diet of the horseshoe bats.

The lesser horseshoe bat, *Rhinolophus hipposideros*, is also of great concern to conservationists, as it is dying out in many areas and becoming rare where it still can be found. One conservation organization in the UK is so worried that it is buying up roost sites of this species in Britain and Ireland in order to protect them. The Irish population is still fairly large and researchers are trying to work out why the declines are occurring elsewhere.

THE FLOWER-FACED BAT

Anthops ornatus is a leaf-nosed bat endemic to the Solomon Islands. It is medium sized, with a 5 cm (2 in) forearm, and is a most attractive bat, with its strikingly ornate orange nose-leaf and silver-and-black fur. There have been only five or so records of this rare bat over the last 100 years. In 1995, a team of zoologists looking for rare bats on Choiseul, one of the bigger islands of the Solomons, eventually caught an individual of this species and managed to obtain the first photograph of the living creature. Tragically, deforestation is likely to reduce the population still further and extinction of this beautiful bat in the near future is a strong possibility.

BELOW The flower-faced bat, *Anthops ornatus*, is one of the rarest bats in the world.

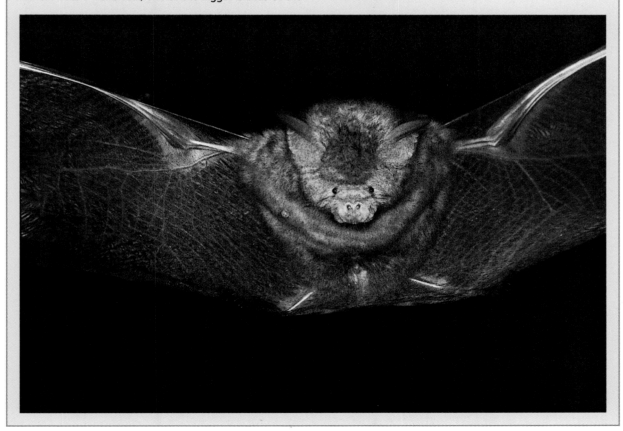

OLD WORLD LEAF-NOSED BATS

About 81 species make up the Family Hipposideridae, the Old World leaf-nosed bats. They are found within the tropics and subtropics from Africa to Australia. They are distinguished by their common name as Old World because there is another family of bats in America with leaf-noses.

Old World leaf-nosed bats are very similar to the horseshoe bats and some authorities think that they should be grouped within that family. There are some subtle distinctions in the skeletal structure between the two (such as the number of bones in the toes), but the most obvious differences are in the shape and form of the nose leaf. There is no sella, the middle part between the horseshoe shape and the lancet of horseshoe bats. Also, the horseshoe shape often has extra leaflets branching off it. The equivalent of the horseshoe bats' lancet is a bulbous projection that is usually rounded. In some species it has small spikes along the top and often has a number of indentations in its face instead of the single, upright, triangular spike of horseshoe bats. The nose-leafs can, however, be very simple.

The shape of the nose-leaf is a useful feature for helping bat researchers to distinguish one species from another. Its prime function is sound emission for their echolocation systems, as these bats, like the horseshoe bats, emit their high-frequency pulses from their nostrils. Some use very high-frequency sounds; one species in India produces sounds over 200 kHz in frequency.

This family includes one of the biggest microbats in the world, the African Commerson's leaf-nosed bat, *Hipposideros commersoni*, with a forearm of

OPPOSITE The orange leaf-nosed bat, *Rhinonycteris aurantius*, is endemic to Australia. It feeds on flying termites in the wet season, but eats moths at other times.

LEFT The fulvous leaf-nosed bat, *Hipposideros fulvus*, endemic to the Indian subcontinent, roosts in cool, damp places.

ABOVE The great Himalayan leaf-nosed bat, *Hipposideros armiger*, found from southern China to Malaysia, hunts low above the ground in open areas among trees.

11 cm (4.3 in) and a 60 cm (2 ft) wingspan. Fur colours in different species range from pale brown to orange. A number of species have two colour phases; in some, males and females are sexually dimorphic, with differently coloured fur. The colourful orange leaf-nosed bat, *Rhinonycteris aurantius*, of Australia, with its beautiful golden fur, is thought by many to be the prettiest bat of that continent.

All Old World leaf-nosed bats are insect-eaters, mostly catching their prey in flight. Some specialize in hunting down cicadas, detecting the sounds these insects give out and homing in on them. As with horseshoe bats, roost sizes can vary, with large roosts containing up to 500,000 individuals, as in *Hipposideros caffer* in Africa. Roosts are often found in caves and other underground sites.

VAMPIRES AND RELATIVES

The New World leaf-nosed bats, the Phyllostomidae, are very different from their Old World relatives just described. They are to be found in the tropical and subtropical parts of America and the Caribbean and include about 160 species. Their most remarkable feature is the huge variety of species. The diversity of habitats available on the American continent has allowed this family to evolve and fit into a large number of niches, including some into which other bats elsewhere in the world have not yet fitted.

These bats, all in a single family, take almost every type of food known to be eaten by bats, including nectar, fruit, mammals, birds, frogs and blood, as well as the more usual microbat diet of insects. This family includes what is arguably the world's biggest microbat, the American false vampire bat, *Vampyrum spectrum*, with a wingspan of about 1 m (3 ft 3 in), and also the best-known bats in the world, the true vampire bats.

Generalizing about this disparate group of bats is difficult. The nose-leaf is not present in all species and it is not as well developed in those that have it as in the leaf-nosed bats of the Old World. Some species in the genus *Phyllostomus* do have quite a large and obvious nose-leaf shaped like a spike (their common name of spear-nosed bats describes them well). Another group, the sword-nosed bats, *Lonchorhina*, have their spike-shaped nose-leaf almost as long as their big ears. Those species of New World leaf-nosed bats that have no proper nose-leafs have

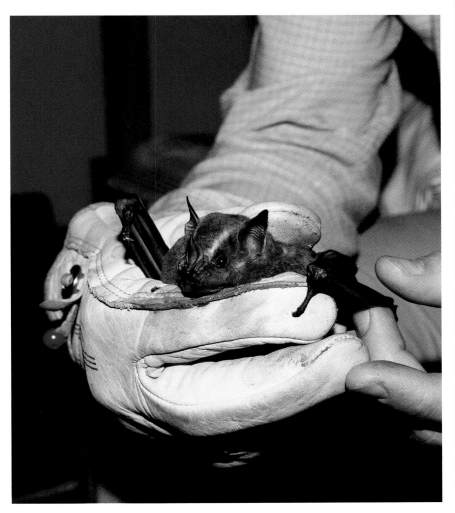

LEFT The great fruit-eating bat, *Artibeus lituratus*, tends to roost in small numbers and has been found under the leaves of coconut palms.

RIGHT Male Seba's short-tailed fruit bats, *Carollia perspicillata*, such as this one, warble greetings to females in their harems.

a strange plate-like growth on the bottom lip instead. These bats have a tragus, another difference from the Old World leaf-nosed bats. As with the latter, the nose-leaf is linked to sound emissions as these bats emit sounds for echolocation through their nostrils, too.

Roosting sites include the hideaways mentioned before, but some members of this family roost in fairly exposed places, such as among foliage. These bats can also be found on buildings, for example tucked under the roof of a veranda, sheltered from the tropical rain but quite exposed to view. Other typical sites include the storm-water drains that run under roads and tracks.

NECTAR, POLLEN AND FRUIT-EATERS

Almost all of the many species in the family Phyllostomidae will eat insects, but a large number have evolved to take other foods, especially fruits, to a greater or lesser extent; they are the New World microbat equivalents of the fruit bats of the Old World. The numerous genera of long-nosed bats in the sub-family Glossophaginae have a long snout that houses an extended tongue. This has a tiny brush-like tip, just like that in the blossom bats, *Syconycteris*, of the megabat family, that is used to gather nectar and pollen as the tongue penetrates deep into flowers. Some species can hover in front of the plant when feeding.

These bats unwittingly transfer pollen on their foreheads and faces to other flowers and act as pollinators. As with the megabats that feed on nectar and pollen, the bats and some of the plants that they feed on have evolved together, so that

the plant provides the food and the bat the means of pollination and seed dispersal. About 500 plant species are pollinated in this way. The bats also eat fruit, and in doing so ingest some seeds, which they deposit in their droppings elsewhere in the forest, so propagating the plant and helping to regenerate the forest.

The short-tailed leaf-nosed bats of the small sub-family Carolliinae have a shorter, more normal-sized muzzle and principally eat fruits, such as figs, *Ficus,* and pepper plants, *Piper.* They have also been seen taking nectar and some eat insects, too. These bats seem to be found everywhere in the Neotropics. Colonies are found in the buildings of villages, and unfortunately often feed at the most convenient places, the cultivated fruit plantations of the villagers, where they take such fruits as coffee, pawpaws, mangoes and bananas, causing them to be regarded as pests.

VALUABLE POLLINATORS

Some of the nectar-feeding phyllostomids, such as the lesser long-nosed bat, *Leptonycteris curasoae*, feed from the flowers of cacti and agaves. These bats are found from the southwestern USA to Central America and northern South America. They migrate south after spending summer in the USA and arrive back in spring, and follow the flowering of the agaves. Migrating bats were found to be drinking sugar water from feeders set out by people to attract hummingbirds. The need to

ABOVE Pallas's long-tongued bat, *Glossophaga soricina*, feeds on insects and fruit as well as nectar.

refill the feeders in the early morning before the birds were active had puzzled the local residents, and led to thoughts of night spirits at work, until bats were seen to be the culprits.

The flowers of some of the agaves open only at night, just to attract bats. In return, they are pollinated by the pollen picked up by the bat on its furry face when it visited the previous blooms. Each bat may visit 100 flowers in the course of a single night. The fruit develops and bats may visit again, taking away the fruit and depositing the seeds elsewhere. Some of these then germinate and so further perpetuate the plants.

Some typical desert plants, such as saguaro and organ pipe cacti, flourish only because of bat pollinators and seed dispersers. One of the agaves is used to make tequila, the spirit drink of Mexico and the surrounding area. The bats have been the main pollinator for this plant, although more recently the plants have been specially cultivated. It is this intimate association between bats and plants that we have to thank for this drink.

BELOW This lesser long-nosed bat, *Leptonycteris curasoae*, is bathed in pollen as it feeds at a saguaro cactus flower, a plant species reliant on the bats for pollination.

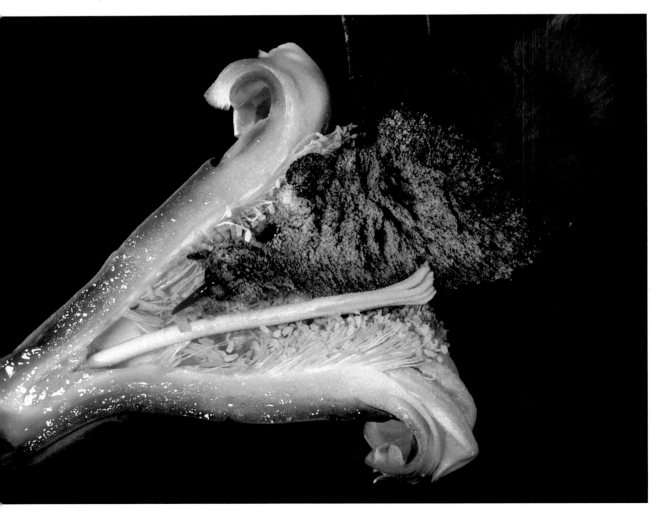

FRUIT EATING

The common fruit bat, *Artibeus jamaicensis*, is one of the most studied of the New World fruit-eating bats. Researchers have found that small native figs make up a large proportion of its diet, but these become scarce at the end of the rainy season, so then the bats move on to palm nuts, avocados and mangoes, and may also try other cultivated fruits.

This is always a difficult time for the bats, and probably limits the population size of this species. During times of plenty, each 50 g (1.8 oz) bat may eat five to ten figs a night, about 50 g (1.8 oz) in total. Food passes through the bats' digestive system very quickly, often in less than 20 minutes. Obtaining enough fruit is always a bit of a struggle. On some fig trees, all the fruits ripen simultaneously, so competition is great because a host of birds, monkeys and other mammals come along for the feast, and there may also be thousands of bats feeding together on the tree as well.

The fruits of other fig trees ripen at different times over a period of weeks, so at any time there are always some ready to eat. However, finding the latter type of tree is not easy, and there is less food to take at each tree. The advantage is that there is less competition.

LEFT The common fruit bat, *Artibeus jamaicensis*, roosts in harems of about ten females with a male.

DISTINCTIVE LOOKS

The white-lined, tent-building, yellow-eared bats of the sub-family Stenodermatinae often have a distinctive pattern on their upper fur. A pair of long white stripes runs from the nose, over the eyes and behind the ears, and another pair runs across the cheeks to the bases of the ears. A single white dorsal stripe runs all the way down the middle of the back. This attractive pattern helps break up the outline of the bat when it roosts in exposed positions outdoors.

These bats are fruit-eaters, although some species also take insects at certain times of the year. Like many of the members of the large family Phyllostomidae, they form harems, with a male standing guard over up to 20 females. They

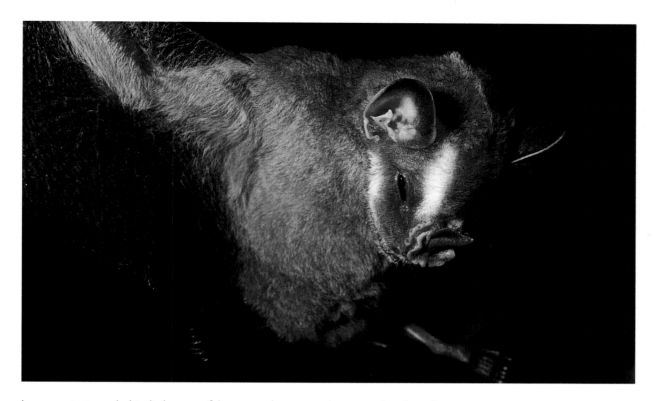

hang up in trees behind clusters of leaves and some make tents. Another close relative that is also a tent-builder, the white bat, *Ectophylla alba*, is white all over (see also p.21). This and a number of other species in the family Phyllostomidae adapt their day roosts to make them more suitable. These bats roost under the shelter of large leaves and use their teeth to nibble the side veins of the leaf so that it collapses downwards from the main stem, wrapping around the bats and giving them more protection. Interestingly, this trick has been evolved by no less than 15 species, including the two *Uroderma* species known as tent-building bats and several *Artibeus* species.

Closely related and looking very similar to the white-lined fruit bats are about 20 species of Neotropical fruit bats *Artibeus*. The sizes vary with a range of forearm lengths from 3.5 cm (1.4 in) to 7.5 cm (3 in). Their facial stripes are narrower and they have no white line down the back. Again, fruit is the main diet; these bats seem to be particularly fond of figs.

FALSE VAMPIRES AND RELATIVES

There are some species in the family Phyllostomidae that are carnivorous as well as taking insects and fruit. They are big enough to catch and kill small vertebrates. Peters' woolly false vampire bat, *Chrotopterus auritus*, and the American false vampire bat, *Vampyrum spectrum*, catch other bats, opossums, mice, birds and amphibians. The American false vampire is one of the world's biggest microbats, with a wingspan of over 90 cm (35 in). Another big phyllostomid bat is the greater spear-nosed bat, *Phyllostomus hastatus*, which occasionally catches small vertebrates as well as insects.

ABOVE The great stripe-faced bat, *Vampyrodes caraccioli*, roosts under palm leaves in small numbers.

OPPOSITE The white bat, *Ectophylla alba*, constructs a tent-like roost from a leaf by nibbling the midrib to make it collapse.

One of the most interesting of the carnivorous members of this family is the fringe-lipped bat, *Trachops cirrhosus*, which specializes in catching frogs. *Trachops* has become well known to biologists after some pioneering studies showed that it listened in to frogs' mating calls so it could identify the non-poisonous species and know their exact location, then swoop in and snatch them. The frogs face a dilemma: if they croak they have a chance of attracting a mate, but they also face the risk of being eaten by a patrolling *Trachops*.

ABOVE Peters' woolly false vampire bat, *Chrotopterus auritus*, roosts in caves, hollow trees and even Mayan ruins, often singly.

RIGHT The fringe-lipped bat, *Trachops cirrhosus*, is a specialist feeder that includes large numbers of frogs in its diet.

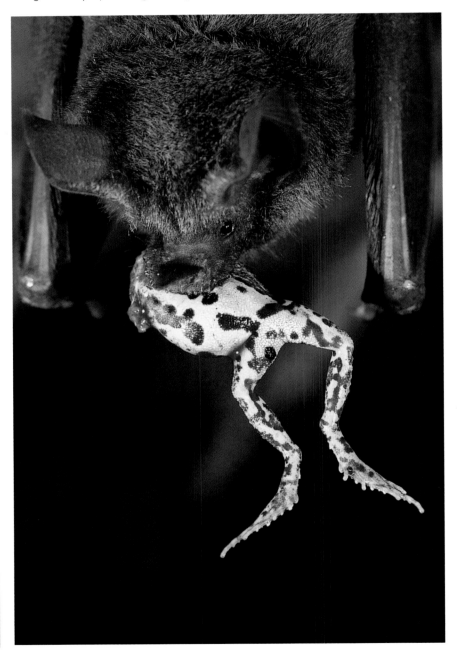

GROTESQUE FEATURES

Beauty is in the eye of the beholder, but there are some very weird-looking members of the Phyllostomidae, even if the beholder is a bat-lover. *Sphaeronycteris toxophyllum* is one of the oddest. It has a protruding brow of skin that extends forward like a roof over its nostrils, and also a flap of loose skin on its chin. *Sphaeronycteris* can sink its head into this lower flap so that the flap meets the protruding forehead. Its face then all but disappears from view, apart from its eyes which can just be seen peeking out through a visor-like slit.

However, the first prize for bizarre looks goes to the wrinkle-faced bat, *Centurio senex*. It has no real muzzle and viewed sideways-on, its face looks almost flat-fronted. Also, it is covered in folds of skin and strange growths. Again, this species can cover its face with loose folds of skin from its chin. These loose folds have a couple of thinner patches covering the eyes, which presumably allow it to see out to some degree. Its wings are adorned with a partially transparent lattice pattern between the fifth and fourth fingers. This is just the sort of species that a bat researcher could spend a lifetime studying to discover all the fascinating reasons why it has these odd features.

LEFT The common vampire bat, *Desmodus rotundus*, is perhaps one of the most persecuted bats in the world.

BIG EARS

The Californian leaf-nosed bat, *Macrotus californicus*, has evolved a range of specializations to find its food and survive in a hostile environment. It lives in the southwestern USA and in northwestern Mexico all year round, uniquely for a member of the Phyllostomidae.

Members of this family cannot hibernate, so other species that live in the area move south for winter. *Macrotus*, however, relies on geothermally heated caves and mines to survive the colder months. It has big ears, nearly half the length of its body, which it uses to listen for the sounds made by grasshoppers and beetles for example, such as the beating of wings as they fly or the rustling as they move around on the ground. Large eyes give these bats excellent night vision for pinpointing their prey. In addition, they probably use echolocation to distinguish insects on foliage.

THE TRUTH ABOUT VAMPIRES

And so to the vampires. Every bat book always includes the vampire bats as do many horror stories, notably the famous novel *Dracula* by Bram Stoker, first published in 1897. So many myths have sprung up surrounding these three species, it is hardly surprising that they create great interest. It is of course their unusual diet that is the chief point of interest; they are the only species of mammal to feed exclusively on blood. Sometimes, a vampire bat will land gently on the back of its selected host, such as a cow or horse, but on other occasions it may alight a little way from the animal and carefully approach it, as vampires are agile bats on the ground, using their feet and thumbs to walk rapidly.

When the bat is on its host, a heat-sensing organ on its face helps it to choose the best place to cut, usually where the blood vessels are close to the surface. The common vampire bat, *Desmodus rotundus*, selects large mammals such as cattle, horses, pigs, sea lions, and very occasionally humans. The other two, much rarer, species the white-winged vampire bat, *Diaemus youngi*, and hairy-legged vampire bat, *Diphylla ecaudata*, tend to prefer blood from wild birds and domestic fowl.

KEEPING THE BLOOD FLOWING

A vampire bat uses its extremely sharp front teeth like razors to slice painlessly into a piece of warm flesh, and a specially evolved tongue enables it to lap a trickle of blood into its mouth. As it feeds, it introduces some anticoagulant into the wound

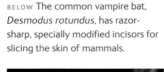

BELOW The common vampire bat, *Desmodus rotundus*, has razor-sharp, specially modified incisors for slicing the skin of mammals.

so that the blood does not clot. The bat quickly processes the large blood meal in its digestive system and urinates to get rid of the water it contains, so that it is not too heavy to take off. The fear of this species arises partly because of the anticoagulant: when the bat has finished, the blood continues to flow and smears a large area, making the damage look far worse than it really is. Another worry results from the fact that the disease rabies can be spread by these bats, but their scarcity limits this problem.

CO-OPERATIVE LIFESTYLE

The fully-fed vampire bats return to their roost sites and, if there is another member of their roost that has not gone out to feed or failed to find a meal, then it is fed by one of the successful bats by regurgitation. Because of their diet and their energy needs, vampire bats have a very finely balanced energy budget; if they do not feed for two or three days, they die of starvation. On any night almost 10% fail to feed, and being able to take food from a successful feeder is how they survive as a species. If only close relatives fed the unsuccessful one, there would be times when none had been successful and they would starve, so this method relies on unrelated bats, too.

There is the problem of freeloaders, vampire bats that have fed and still want more if they can get it. However, it seems that vampire bats recognize each other and know which individuals are cheating and which are likely to reciprocate in the future, so some get refused. Many other animals will give food to their own young or mate, but not to unrelated animals. The example of true altruism demonstrated by the vampire bats is very, very rare in the natural world.

SUFFERING PERSECUTION

Prompted by their fear of these bats, worried local people have been known to dynamite caves of roosting bats, wrongly thinking they were vampires. In reality, vampire bats are far from the powerful, terrifying monsters of the human imagination. They are small bats, with forearm lengths of only 5.5 cm (2.2 in) and a combined body-and-head length of 8 cm (3.1 in). Mosquitoes are far, far more dangerous as they not only drink human blood, but are found all over the world in infinitely greater numbers and cause major health problems by spreading various devastating diseases, such as malaria and yellow fever.

The persecution of vampire bats has been so great that they have become rare in some areas. Their range is restricted to parts of Trinidad, Central America and the northern part of South America (and they have never occurred in Transylvania!).

CHAPTER 5
Microbats II

H AVING LOOKED AT SOME of the microbats with strange front ends, we now look at some with strange back ends, and even some which look quite normal, such is the wide variation in the designs of the microbat families.

OPPOSITE Lesser long-eared bat, *Nyctophilus geoffroyi*, Tasmania, Australia.

TAILED BATS

Although many microbats have an interfemoral membrane (or uropatagium) joining the tail to the hindlimbs, the tails of some species are free, like those of most mammals. The following section to p.96 takes a look at some of the families of microbats with strange tails.

THE SHEATH-TAILED FAMILY

The tails of the sheath-tailed bats (Family Emballonuridae) are set partly within the tail membrane in a sheath at the base. The free portion of the tail can protrude out of this little protective pocket and appear on the top surface of the membrane. What could be the advantage of this odd arrangement? One theory is that when these bats fly, they stretch out their legs and the membrane slides along the tail so that it can serve a variety of functions, for example as a rudder or an insect-catching scoop. At such times, the tail bone would give the membrane strength. At rest the membrane could slide up to the base of the tail and give the bat more mobility, using its back legs and partly free tail.

There are about 50 species of these strange-tailed bats and they can be found in the tropics worldwide. All have long, narrow wings that enable them to fly fast, and they usually stay high in the sky, which is a sensible precaution against possible collision with branches or other obstacles when travelling at speed. Many have forward-pointing ears to help with streamlining. At rest their leathery wings are so long that they have an extra fold.

Some sheath-tailed bats have two white lines down their backs and four species are all-white. This unusual fur colour probably camouflages them as they roost beneath leaves (see also p.21).

ABOVE This black-bearded tomb bat, *Taphozous melanopogon*, has its tail unsheathed.

BELOW Bats in the family Emballonuridae, such as this Raffray's sheath-tailed bat, *Emballonura raffrayana*, have simple, plain faces.

SAC-WINGED BATS

Various species of sheath-tailed bats have extra oddities. The sac-winged bats of the genera *Saccolaimus* and *Taphozous*, found from Africa to southern Asia and Australia, have a small pouch, or sac, on each wing, near the shoulder. These sacs are used to collect secretions from the genitalia that then ferment inside them. The strong-smelling product is probably used for attracting mates, marking others in the colony or the roost site, or all of these purposes. The sacs on males are more developed than those on females, so sex is likely to be involved. Species in the genus *Taphozous* have a gland on the throat, probably also for producing scent, which again is more highly developed in males. They roost in tombs as well as in trees and caves, hence their common name of tomb bats.

THE LONG-NOSED BAT

Perhaps the most peculiar member of this group is the long-nosed (or proboscis) bat, *Rhynchonycteris naso*, which is common along waterways linked to the Amazon and the Orinoco, and also in the surrounding forest. As both the common and scientific names suggest, the animal's snout is long and pointed, making it look as though its lower jaw is too short. These odd bats roost out on tree trunks and branches in exposed positions, but are amazingly well camouflaged against potential predators, with little tufts of hair on their forearms and patterned and grizzled

yellowish and greyish fur. Like other sheath-tailed bats, they have a distinctive posture at rest, being raised up on their wrists with the forearms splayed out and the head held back.

Long-nosed bats usually feed over water, and can be seen roosting on the underside of tree branches overhanging rivers, and are sometimes hard to distinguish from the tufts of lichen and mosses due to the cryptic patterning and colouring on their fur and wings. They roost in small numbers, and often in a line down the underside of the branch with each bat well separated from its neighbour giving all the appearances of bark flaking off the tree or mossy lumps. They are always very alert during the day and difficult to approach without causing them to fly off.

ABOVE These long-nosed bats, *Rhynchonycteris naso*, are superbly camouflaged against a background of lichens and mosses on tree trunks in Costa Rica.

OPPOSITE The free tail of a white-striped mastiff bat, *Tadarida australis*. Most free-tailed bats have a band of skin on the forehead joining the base of the ears.

RIGHT The lesser mouse-tailed bat, *Rhinopoma hardwickii*, usually forms only small roosts of fewer than ten individuals.

MOUSE-TAILED BATS

The mouse-tailed bats (Rhinopomatidae) comprise a much smaller family than the sheath-tails, with only four species, all in the genus *Rhinopoma*. They live from Africa east to Sumatra and Thailand. Their most distinctive feature is the long, whip-like free tail sticking out at the back, which is almost as long as the head and body combined. These bats live in dry areas and have nostrils that they can close by means of flaps of skin, possibly to stop dust blowing in. They also have specially adapted kidneys that enable them to conserve water. Mouse-tailed bats typically roost in caves and among rocks; some are found in Egyptian pyramids, where they have been recorded for millennia. At certain times of the year when food becomes scarce they become torpid and live off a huge amount of store fat.

FREE-TAILED OR MASTIFF BATS

The free-tailed or mastiff bats (Molossidae) is a large family of 100 species that can be found all around the world in a wide band as far north as southern Europe and the central USA, and as far south as southern Australia and almost to the tip of South America.

GUANO FOR FERTILIZER

Caves that are used by large conglomerations of bats produce enough guano (accumulated faeces) each year to make it worth harvesting. The droppings from microbats are rich in nitrates and phosphates and make a good fertilizer. This is then sold to improve food production. In Thailand, for instance, some local people rely on this resource to make their living. They enter the big bat caves periodically to dig out sackfuls of the guano that may lie many feet thick on the ground and sell it to farmers and local growers. They jealously guard the caves and this prevents disturbance of the bats, helping their conservation. At Carlsbad Cavern in New Mexico, USA, at least 40 tonnes of guano used to be extracted daily during the winter months, and this went on for 15 years when the greatest number of bats used the site.

OPPOSITE A small part of a vast roost of Mexican free-tailed bats, *Tadarida brasiliensis*, emerge from Bracken Cave in Texas, USA.

Their tails are stout, and stick out well beyond a short tail membrane. These bats fly high and fast and their sleek, velvety fur provides a streamlined surface. They keep their fur in tip-top condition by grooming and combing it with a thickened outer toe equipped with bristle-like hairs. Their faces are striking, with big ears meeting on top of the head in most species, and rather thick lips, marked in some species with deep, vertical wrinkles.

The common names of the different species in this family are descriptive: there are goblin bats, flat-headed bats, broad-faced bats, big-eared bats, mastiff bats, velvety bats and hairless bats. The last name is given to two species living in the Philippines that are nearly naked, with just the odd tuft of hair on the head and tail. These bats also have a big throat gland that produces extremely pungent scents that are, no doubt, attractive to other bats, and they can pack their wings away in a convenient bag of skin along the sides of their bodies.

Free-tailed bats roost in buildings, caves, rock fissures, trees, indeed, almost anywhere that bats are known to roost. One reason why they are of special interest to humans is because some species gather in huge numbers, up to several million at a time. Their mass exodus is spectacular and can begin early in the afternoon as there are so many bats to emerge (see also box, *Record roosts*, p.33). The vast assemblages create so much guano that it is commercially harvested in some parts of the world. Free-tailed bat guano was even used by the Confederates to make gunpowder during the American Civil War.

MEXICAN FREE-TAILED BATS

The gatherings of Mexican free-tailed bats, *Tadarida brasiliensis*, in their millions at their roosts in caves are one of the wonders of the natural world. In the past, Bracken Cave in Texas, USA, has housed 20 million of these bats. However, numbers have declined in recent years and it is believed that insecticides in the ecosystem are to blame. With such large numbers, the bats have to forage over a huge area to find sufficient food. They have been recorded flying upwards to an altitude of about 3,000 m (10,000 ft) before flying off to their feeding areas, which are up to 50 km (30 miles) away from the roosting caves (see also box *Record roosts*, p.33).

PUNK BAT

Males of the crested mastiff bat, *Chaerephon chapini*, from Africa have elongated hairs on their crowns that stick up in a punk-like crest. Why should creatures that spend so much of their time in darkness have such spectacular ornamentation? The females have a tiny little tuft, but nothing like the dramatic erectile hairpieces of the males. It is assumed that the long hairs of the males help waft the odours from scent glands at their bases.

THE ADVANTAGE OF A FREE TAIL?

So why have free tails when other species tend to have their tails enclosed in membranes of skin? One possible answer to this question comes from a careful piece of observation of European free-tailed bats, *Tadarida teniotis*, returning to

roost between concrete blocks making up the walls of houses in France. The bats were seen to turn around inside the narrow roosting place and back up towards their final resting place, using the tail as a sensitive probe to find the way. This could explain the free-tailed bats' tails being thick and fleshy, as such a tail is likely to be more touch-sensitive. However, a sensory function is not likely to be the explanation for the very thin and long tail of the mouse-tailed bats, *Rhinopoma*. Finding the answer to such unknowns is one of the many delights enjoyed by studying bats.

VESPER BATS

The Vespertilionidae is the biggest and most widespread of all the bat families, with its 400 or so species ranging from the heat of the tropics to the cold winters of the temperate zones. Vesper bats, as they are often known, are found high up mountains where vegetation begins to become scarce, as well as low down in tropical rainforests; they are in deserts, in cities, in woodland and farmland, on islands and inland, in fact everywhere except the coldest regions in high latitudes.

ABOVE Two of the toes of free-tailed bats, such as this black mastiff bat, *Molossus ater*, of Central America, are fattened and covered in tactile bristles, possibly to aid grooming, but their function is as yet unknown.

RIGHT Daubenton's bat, *Myotis daubentonii*, is a medium-sized *Myotis*, with a forearm length of 3.8 cm (1.5 in).

Most of these bats look relatively unremarkable; they have not needed to develop strange-shaped nose-leafs or other facial adornments. All are insect-eaters, which explains their ability to live on every continent in the world, as insects are very widespread, although a select band of species also catch fish. Despite their lack of dramatic distinctive features, these bats all have special lifestyles adapting them for particular niches. However, these are very subtle and take years of study to discover. In many temperate regions vesper bats comprise the main bat populations, although some areas have a few species of horseshoe and free-tailed bats as well.

The relatively plain faces of vesper bats do have a few interesting features. Many have nostrils that protrude slightly, and in some cases a lot. There are lumps and bumps on the muzzles that ooze oil and are probably scent glands. In most species the ears are relatively small, but a few species have huge ears, almost as big as the body. Generally, vesper bats have plain brown or black fur.

ABOVE The Natterer's bat, *Myotis nattereri*, shows the unadorned face typical of the vesper bats. The tragus shape and size are useful identification features.

RIGHT A greater mouse-eared bat, *Myotis myotis*, hibernating in a cave. In summer, roosts of this species can contain up to 2,000 females.

MOUSE-EARED BATS

One genus of the vesper bats is called *Myotis*, which means 'mouse-eared', and this family does have mouse-like ears, but so do many other bats. There are nearly a hundred species of *Myotis* bats and they can be found all over the world, from Europe to Japan, from Africa to Australia, and from Canada to Chile. One species lives on an island south of Tierra del Fuego, while another species has been found just inside the Arctic Circle.

The biggest of the *Myotis* bats, with a forearm length of 6.5 cm (2.6 in), is the greater mouse-eared bat, *Myotis myotis*. It used to have a small population on the south coast of Britain, but this became extinct in 1990 and the species has also declined in numbers over its range in other parts of Europe including Germany and Austria.

WATER SKIMMERS

One of the most attractive and distinctive members of the genus is Daubenton's bat, *Myotis daubentonii*, which has a spectacular feeding method of skimming the surface of still water, such as lakes, and catching insects at the water surface with its large feet. It then reaches down and stuffs the insect into its mouth, all while flying along within a few centimetres (about 1 in) of the water. Its shallow wingbeats enable it to fly so low yet avoid hitting the water. This unusual bat takes insects that other bats cannot catch, which reduces inter-species competition. Daubenton's bats have been recorded travelling over 10 km (6 miles) from their roosts to their feeding areas. They navigate by following rivers and canals as we would roads, as well as using them as feeding areas. Daubenton's bats roost in tree cavities, wet tunnels and stone buildings, usually close to water if possible. In spring and summer, females segregate to form a maternity roost of fewer than 200 individuals while the males roost elsewhere, often singly. In winter these bats hibernate underground. A species that looks very similar to Daubenton's bat, but with even bigger feet, is the large-footed myotis, *Myotis adversus*, of Australia. Apart from catching insects from the water surface, this impressive species rakes its toes through the water and grabs small fish. Mexico, too, has a *Myotis* species, *Myotis vivesi*, that catches small fish.

ROOSTING BEHAVIOUR

The little brown bat, *Myotis lucifugus*, is found in Canada and the USA, except for some southern states. For those lucky enough to have bats roosting in their properties, this is one of the species that is most likely to turn up. It prefers buildings close to water, where it can catch large numbers of aquatic insects. In summer, the nursery colonies may contain 500 or more females. Little brown bats are able to withstand very hot conditions in their roost sites, temperatures as high as

BELOW Little brown bats, *Myotis lucifugus*, hibernating. These bats may move more than 300 km (185 miles) in order to find suitable hibernacula.

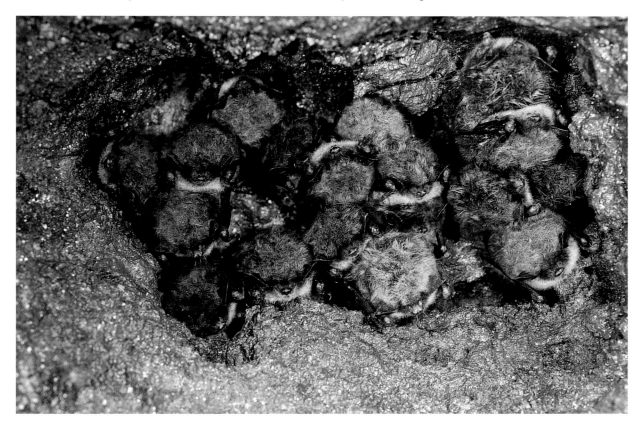

54°C (129°F) have been recorded. They live near marshes and rivers, and mosquitoes, which are a major public nuisance and potential health hazard in such areas, make up an important part of their diet. This fact is used in gaining public and official opinion to help conserve roosts. In winter, little brown bats may travel as far as 320 km (200 miles) to suitable hibernation sites underground.

In winter, *Myotis* bats may congregate in large numbers in favourite caves. Almost all of the grey myotis bats, *Myotis grisescens*, south of Kentucky and east of the Mississippi in the USA, are thought to hibernate in three caves, with over 1.5 million in one cave alone. As with other bat species that hibernate or roost in such great numbers, this makes these bats highly vulnerable should disaster strike, but conservation measures are helping to ensure that no harm befalls this concentrated population.

GAUDY BATS

Painted bats, *Kerivoula*, sometimes called woolly bats, live in Africa and Southeast Asia. These bats fly weakly, low above the ground. They roost outdoors and have remarkable camouflage, with fur colours in shades of red, orange, grey and black. Wings of the painted bat, *Kerivoula picta*, which occurs from India to Indonesia, may be black with orange bands along the line of the fingers or all-orange. Once hanging up in trees, painted bats can look like clumps of moss or dead leaves due to the colour and woolly nature of their fur.

The least forest bat, *Kerivoula minuta*, is only a little bigger than the hog-nosed bat of Thailand, *Craseonycteris thonglongyai*, the smallest bat in the world. North America is home to a very attractive-looking bat, the spotted bat, *Euderma maculatum*, which can be found along the western side of the continent, from Canada south to Mexico. It has black or dark brown fur with huge white spots on its shoulders and rump. This striking pattern and its absolutely huge ears make it a bat to remember, if one can find it as it is rare.

CONFUSING SIMILARITIES

Myotis bats all look very similar to one another, indeed, some are so similar that even bat experts find it difficult to identify them in the field. In Europe, for instance, Brandt's bat, *Myotis brandtii*, is so similar to the whiskered bat, *Myotis mystacinus*, that the two were thought to be a single species until 1958. One of the features used to distinguish them is the shape of the penis.

PIPISTRELLES

As far as hard-to-tell-apart species are concerned, pipistrelles are in a class of their own. They all look extremely similar, and new species are still being distinguished now that DNA testing is available. These are generally small bats, with their fur brown all over. They have a jerky flight, emerge early and feed out in the open so they are easy to see. Like *Myotis* bats, the pipistrelles are widely dispersed around the world, although the New World has only a couple of species. Many species are very small, and the Indian pygmy pipistrelle, *Pipistrellus mimus*, is one of the smallest, with a forearm length of only about 2.7 cm (just over 1 in). There are 77 species worldwide.

LEFT The common pipistrelle, *Pipistrellus pipistrellus*, showing the short, blunt tragus. Pipistrelles also have a post-calcarial lobe, unlike many other vesper bats.

ROOSTING HABITS

In Britain, modern houses have become the commonest summer roosting site for the common pipistrelle, *Pipistrellus pipistrellus*, and the recently distinguished soprano pipistrelle, *Pipistrellus pygmaeus*. They seem to appreciate the warmth and clean conditions provided in the eaves, and maternity roosts of as many as 1,000 females have been recorded in such sites.

The fact that pipistrelles have learned to live in close proximity to humans has unwittingly proved to be a successful move in terms of their survival. The females often move around between roost sites, sometimes splitting up between two or three sites, sometimes joining together at one. Even when they have given birth, they may still fly from place to place, carrying their youngsters with them on their undersides. The advantage to the bats is that no one can work out where the roost has moved to, although this can prove frustrating for bat biologists.

In winter, common and soprano pipistrelles will hibernate in fairly exposed sites such as at a cave entrance, around a poorly fitting window frame or behind window shutters, for instance. They are rarely found underground, yet in the USA and Canada the eastern pipistrelle, *Pipistrellus subflavus*, hibernates in caves. Unlike the European species, these bats roost in summer only in small numbers,

BELOW Common pipistrelles, *Pipistrellus pipistrellus*, flying in a house roof space. This species has benefited by living close to humans.

in rock crevices, caves and even among clumps of Spanish moss, *Tillandsia*. They are unusual among bats in that the females seem to regularly produce twins. An African species, *Pipistrellus nanus*, is called the banana bat, as it can often be found roosting in curled-up banana leaves. Although they look so similar, it is clear that pipistrelles show a wide range of behaviour, providing plenty of questions for bat researchers to answer.

UNUSUAL HIDING PLACES

The bamboo or club-footed bats, *Tylonycteris*, of Southeast Asia have extremely flattened skulls and suction pads on their feet and wrists. These small bats roost inside hollow bamboo stems that they enter through narrow holes made by beetle larvae. The narrow skull allows them to squeeze inside and the suction pads help them obtain a grip on a joint in the bamboo stem when roosting. There is no way in for any predator. The narrow-winged bat, *Mimetillus*, of Africa has similar features, and roosts behind dead bark on trees. It has short wings that it has to beat very fast to stay aloft, and it then needs to rest regularly because it tires quickly.

NOCTULES AND RELATIVES

Closely related to the pipistrelles are the six species of noctules, *Nyctalus*. They look similar, but much bigger. Many have forearm lengths of 5 cm (slightly less than 2 in), compared with those of pipistrelles that average about 3.3 cm (1.3 in). Generally, noctules are forest bats and some roost solely in tree cavities. They have broad muzzles and powerful jaws, ideal for seizing and crunching up big beetles such as cockchafers.

Noctules fly higher than pipistrelles and their bursts of echolocation calls are much louder. Although they are well adapted for catching big insects, some have been found to be eating large numbers of tiny insects, too. Noctules are powerful fliers, and may travel daily over 10 km (6 miles) to feeding areas from their roosts and make long migrations during late August to October.

On summer evenings the noctule bat, *Nyctalus noctula*, of Western Europe has been seen just before dusk, feeding among groups of common swifts, *Apus apus*, on high-flying insects, such as flying ants. This species is often seen hunting just above tree-top height above water such as lakes, canals and rivers. Closely-related Leisler's bats, *Nyctalus leisleri*, have been found roosting in house roofs in Britain and Ireland, just like pipistrelles.

ABOVE Noctule bats, *Nyctalus noctula*, are reliant on tree cavities for roosts, so they have declined in areas where forest practice removes old trees.

SEROTINES

A group allied to the noctules is that of the big brown bats or serotines, *Eptesicus*. The big brown bat, *Eptesicus fuscus*, of America is well-known, due to its use of buildings for roosting. It is commonly found in attics and churches, and roosts have sometimes built up to contain as many as 800 individuals. The serotine bat, *Eptesicus serotinus*, in Western Europe does the same, but the sizes of roosts are usually much smaller. At present, it seems to be suffering a worrying decline in the UK, and well-established roosts are dying out.

RIGHT Big brown bats, *Eptesicus fuscus*, uses buildings to roost in. Here they are roosting in an attic.

LONG-EARED BATS

One of the most spectacular looking groups of vesper bats is that of the long-eared bats, *Plecotus*. Their ears are so long that flying along with them upright would cause problems with aerodynamics. Instead, the bats direct their faces groundwards, so ensuring that the tips of the ears are pointing forward. These bats have openings in the top of the snout, and issue their echolocation calls through these, so that it is directed forwards. When at rest they allow their huge ears to curl down.

These extraordinary ears are used to listen for the sound insects make as they fly or move around on vegetation. They are also used to pick up very quiet echoes bouncing back from the whispers they emit when they echolocate. Some moths, such as noctuids, have evolved 'ears' of their own that are tuned in to the frequency of bat calls, so that they can avoid most bats as they can hear them approaching. They do not hear the long-eared bats, however, and these whispering bats make a living out of catching these moths.

BELOW A group of roosting brown long-eared bats, *Plecotus auritus*, in a house attic. This species usually roosts along the ridge beam.

RIGHT The brown long-eared bat, *Plecotus auritus*, folds its huge ears down when at rest or hibernating.

Thanks to their broad wings, long-eared bats can hover and glean insects from leaves as well as in flight. They are also able to take off from a flat surface, whereas many other species of bats when on the ground have to walk along to a vertical surface and climb up a couple of metres (about 6 feet) before they can launch themselves into flight. In Europe, the summer roosts of brown long-eared bats, *Plecotus auritus*, which tend to be in attics of buildings and church roofs, contain adult males mixed in with the females. This is unusual as in most other vesper bat species the sexes segregate.

In the USA, Townsend's long-eared bat, *Plecotus townsendii*, roosts mainly in caves and mines in maternity roosts of up to 1,000 bats, whereas the European species form roosts of less than 100. In winter, they hibernate in caves and tuck their long ears back along the side of their heads and bodies, under their wings. They have a couple of glandular swellings on the snout that ooze yellowish oil. This is either for keeping their fur and skin in good condition or for scent-marking, or both.

BENT-WINGED BATS

Bent-winged bats, *Miniopterus*, have especially long third fingers on their wings, and when at rest they fold the outer quarter of each of these long wings inwards. They like their own company and roosts of tens of thousands in caves are not unusual. One species, Schreibers' bent-winged bat, *Miniopterus schreibersii*, has a very wide distribution, extending from southwest Europe east to China and south to Australia and some of the Pacific islands. Interestingly, in the tropics, their babies begin to develop as soon as the females are mated, whereas in the temperate zones

LEFT Schreibers' bent-winged bat, *Miniopterus schreibersii*, showing the characteristically folded wing. These bats can form very large roosts.

they practice delayed implantation, in which the fertilized egg is not immediately implanted onto the uterus wall (see also p.36). Their long wings enable them to fly fast, and speeds up to 50 km/hr (30 mph) have been recorded.

CHAPTER 6
Bat conservation

BATS ARE UNDER THREAT IN MANY AREAS of the world. Some have declined to such an extent that the numbers remaining may not be enough to sustain the species. Some species, such as the Guam flying fox, *Pteropus tokudae*, the Puerto Rican flower bat, *Phyllonycteris major*, and the New Zealand greater short-tailed bat, *Mystacina robusta*, have become extinct in recent times. Species most at risk are those living in isolation and those living at low densities; any changes to their environment could wipe out the species. Some fruit bats on isolated Pacific and Indian Ocean islands, such as the Comoro black flying fox, *Pteropus livingstonii*, and the Marianas flying fox, *Pteropus mariannus*, are at great risk of extinction. Some microbats living in one small area are also threatened such as the Kitti's hog-nosed bat, *Craseonycteris thonglongyai*, on the Thai-Burmese border.

OPPOSITE Schreibers' bent-winged bat, *Miniopterus schreibersii*, roosting in a cave, France. Note the ring.

BELOW The great golden-crowned flying fox, *Acerodon jubatus*, one of the biggest bats in the world. Populations of this and other species of bats are being seriously affected by humans in some areas of the world.

BIODIVERSITY AND FOOD CHAINS

Threats to bat populations matters not just because bats are fascinating creatures in their own right. Our increasing familiarity with the term biodiversity from television, newspapers, magazines and other media reflects the importance biologists place on this aspect of conservation. They are realizing that the more diversity there is in animal and plant populations, then the healthier is the environment.

The easiest way to appreciate what is involved is to recall the concept of food chains and webs from biology lessons at school. It all starts with the producers, the plants that manufacture the food in their leaves by photosynthesis. Animals such as caterpillars then join the chain and eat the leaves, other animals such as birds eat the caterpillars, and so on up the chain. If a species dies out, then there is a break in the chain, and predators that relied on that species could also die or grow weaker as there is less food available. If, like the microbats, an animal is at the end of the food chain and it becomes extinct, then the creatures that it preyed upon will increase in number and compete with others for food and space, so upsetting other food chains.

The fruit bats and some microbats have an even more direct effect. By pollinating plants and dispersing their seeds in the course of feeding, they ensure the survival of many species of trees and other plants and the recolonization of cleared forest. So we have more diversity, but how does it affect us humans? Many of us have become so used to hunting and gathering our food from supermarket shelves rather than in the forests that we forget about the vital importance of food chains. All our food is reliant on plants, and the plants are mostly reliant on animal visitors to pollinate them, creatures such as bees, birds and bats that are all part of food chains.

MAINTAINING A BALANCE

There is another important point, a single insect-eating bat may eat hundreds of insects a night, and there are few other nocturnal insect-eaters. Most birds for instance, feed in the daytime on a different set of day-flying insects. Take away a small roost of a hundred bats and there will be a large number of extra insects flitting around the area each night. So bats help to keep a balance in the natural world. Furthermore, they are a great help to humans, as farmland, gardens and house timbers all suffer attacks from insect pests and bats are instrumental in keeping down their numbers.

HANDS-ON CONSERVATION

One of the most effective steps people can take to help microbats is to increase the number of roosting sites available to them.

BAT BOXES OR BAT HOUSES

Installing bat roosting boxes, similar to bird nest-boxes but with a narrow entrance underneath rather than a hole in the front, helps increase the number of roosting

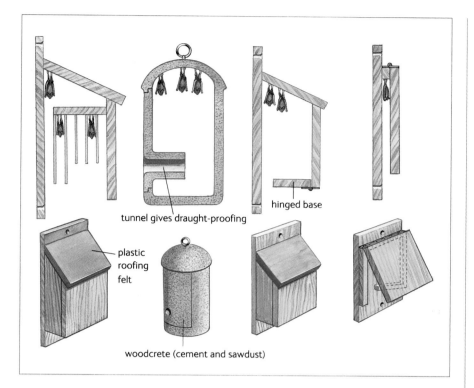

tunnel gives draught-proofing

hinged base

plastic roofing felt

woodcrete (cement and sawdust)

Bat roosting boxes can be of different designs to suit different species.

BELOW Bat roosting boxes are a valuable and easy way to monitor bat populations in woodlands.

sites. The size and design need to be tailored to different species, but as long as the bat can crawl from the entrance upwards and hang in a sheltered, dry place in darkness at the top then it should be suitable. Bat boxes are of particular importance in areas such as coniferous woodland, or deciduous woodland where mature trees with holes and hollows are cut down, which contain few or no natural roosting places.

Basically the bat needs to be able to crawl in through a narrow gap, then crawl up to roost out of the draught of the opening. Some species, such as pipistrelles, prefer to squeeze into a roost, so partitions inside may help. Wood is easy to shape, but no preservatives should be used in case they affect the sensitive bats. Boxes made of woodcrete (a mixture of sawdust and cement) last much longer and provide higher humidity levels in summer. Bat houses should be erected on trees or high posts facing different directions to provide variable temperature roosts, and as high as is possible. Strips of carpet wrapped around the trunk of a tree and tacked to it at the top have worked, as have corrugated iron bands and plain boards. Bats have even been found roosting between the bat box and the tree and not using the box itself!

PROVIDING GARDEN ATTRACTIONS

If you want bats to visit your garden, then some habitat management may be in order. Try planting shrubs, such as jasmines and honeysuckles, which give off scents at night. The scent attracts night-flying insects and these in turn attract the bats. Insects build up in number where there is shelter, so ensure there is a high hedge or fence or even a row of conifers to protect the garden from the prevailing winds. A garden pond acts like a magnet to insects and bats will feed over it and sometimes swoop down for a drink, too. If you have one, turn on the security light or other outdoor illumination and insects will be attracted, and then the bats will come to feed.

COUNTRYSIDE MANAGEMENT FOR BATS

Similar habitat management on a much larger scale is starting to happen in state-controlled woodlands, where maintenance of firebreaks throughout the wood is linked to insect conservation. Mowing is carried out at certain times linked to insect breeding cycles, and the edges of firebreaks are allowed to grow up a little to add extra diversity. Insect numbers increase and the bats can obtain plenty of food along these avenues.

Tree planting is being linked more to conservation rather than to just providing a commercial resource, so native trees are being replaced when non-native ones are harvested. Old, dying trees are no longer grubbed out, but allowed to rot slowly and provide a whole range of insects that recycle the wood and are, in turn, recycled by the bats. Also the bats can continue to use rot-holes for roosting.

Farming practices are being slowly changed to help wildlife, too. In Europe, subsidies are being given to allow some farmland to remain fallow. There is more financial encouragement to plant hedgerows and laws are now in place to protect old hedgerows after decades of hedgerow removal to increase field size for more efficient crop production. Bats use hedgerows as route-ways to their feeding areas and find more insects where native flowers have been allowed to grow around field edges and in fallow ground. Many farmers are becoming more aware of the benefits of working with nature. The hedgerows provide some shelter from the wind and help prevent soil erosion, and the increased number of insects helps with pollination of some crops.

BIODIVERSITY AGREEMENTS

In Europe, biodiversity agreements have resulted in the feeding areas of some of the rarer bats being protected. This means that huge areas of the landscape are managed in a better way for bats and no undesirable influence is allowed to impinge. Some of the horseshoe bats are protected in this way.

CREATING HIBERNACULA

In temperate climates the importance of hibernation sites is well known to bat conservationists. In the UK some bat workers have embarked on the major project of building tunnels to serve as hibernacula for bats. Huge constructions of large concrete pipes angling into the ground for 20 m (65 ft) or more, and covered with a thick layer of insulating soil. Some of these pioneering conservationists have dug into chalk cliff faces and made caverns suitable for the species in the area.

One of the biggest and most ambitious of such schemes to date was built around a pre-existing mine where the air flow was slow, so that any hot air from summer would not allow the cold air of winter to flow in and make it suitable for bats. A

LEFT This purpose-made bat brick in the roof of a hibernaculum is being used by two brown long-eared bats, *Plecotus auritus*, and a Natterer's bat, *Myotis nattereri*.

BELOW Improving a hibernaculum by reducing the flow of air through a disused railway tunnel.

local enthusiast decided to build a two-storey concrete building over the entrance and paint parts of it black. During the day the black absorbed the heat from outside and warmed the air inside. This warm air rose and caused circulation around the whole tunnel system, creating a natural air-conditioning system. In addition, summer roosting places were made available for bats in the outside structure. The numbers of bats using the tunnel in winter has increased dramatically since the work, and no

ABOVE Grilles like this allow bats access into underground sites, but exclude humans.

less than ten of Britain's 16 resident species of bats are now found there.

As well as improving such sites by modifying the air flow, which can alter the humidity as well as the temperatures within them, hibernacula can also be greatly enhanced by providing more hanging places for the bats. Many wartime bunkers have been turned into excellent hibernacula by covering them with about 1 m (3 ft 3 in) of earth to insulate them. Disused railway tunnels make good sites, but have too much air blowing through them, so blocking one end creates a more stable environment. Modifications such as these need to be carried out with official authority approval and with full agreement from statutory nature conservation bodies. It is too easy to mean well, but find that your adjustments have made the site excellent for a locally common species and useless for the national rarity that used to occur there!

Perhaps the quickest and greatest improvement that can be made to hibernacula is by preventing human access. Some people love to explore underground and they can, by accident or design, inflict damage on roosting bats. Hibernating bats will begin to arouse if the temperature changes by less than 1 °C (1.8 °F). A person standing under a hibernating bat will warm it more than that. As one moves underground, the air is disturbed and warmer air may be wafted onto bats hibernating in a colder area.

Bats are disturbed by noise, too, and not just by sounds such as talking or banging against rocks. They are especially sensitive to high-frequency sounds, and so will be upset by such noises as the rustling of a nylon anorak or the clinking of coins, which give out high-frequency sounds as well as noises we can hear.

Bats in hibernation survive by slowly burning up stored fat. By the end of the winter all of this fat will be used up and, hopefully, insects will be flying again. However, when bats are disturbed during hibernation, they begin to burn up more of their precious fat in order to wake and move to a safer, quieter place. If they suffer too many disturbances, bats will die of starvation.

Erecting horizontal bars across entrances will allow access for the bats, but keep the public out, as long as the bars are the correct distance apart. Usually a gate is included, so that bat surveyors can enter and check all is well each year. Serious cavers should not be excluded from their hobby, but there will be times when the bats are in residence when it is better to avoid entering a site. Close liaison with the cavers is important as they often have plenty of knowledge of the best underground sites for bats. Putting up a noticeboard explaining why the site is closed off may prevent the vandalism that sadly has sometimes been inflicted on such gates.

PROTECTING ROOSTS IN HOUSES AND OTHER SITES

Much success has been achieved in protecting bats that are roosting in houses in Europe and the USA by talking to the house-owners and asking them to look after their guests in the attic. After a little education about the importance of bats and the struggle they have in life, many owners are only too happy to help and will carry out annual counts to monitor population levels.

Sooner or later, buildings used as bat roosts need repair. If the work is carried out with care, both the site and the bats can be saved. The bats tend to roost in such places for only part of the year, so there is likely to be a time when there will be none present to disturb. The basic conditions of the existing roost can be copied in the renovations, such as a similar size entrance slit in the same place, the same roosting area and no obstructions outside the entrance. Sometimes, parts of the old timbers can be re-used by the roost's entrance so the new home smells familiar to the bats.

In England any remedial work on ancient parish churches around the country first requires a report from a church architect. After lobbying from bat conservationists, bats were included on the official report form, so if signs of bats are present then the correct authorities must be notified before work can commence. Including an extra tick box on the forms has meant that hundreds of bat roosts have been saved each year.

BELOW A problem solved! Bat droppings from the eaves roost no longer land on the balcony as they are deflected by the board above the doorway.

In some countries, sites may be protected to help the local employment situation. As well as the importance of the roosts in large bat caves to guano miners there is an increasing tourist industry springing up around spectacular bat roosts (see p.33). The huge roosts of free-tailed bats are so stunning that tourists happily find them included in their itinerary. The roosting caves in Texas and New Mexico are world-famous and now geared up to cater for thousands of visitors a week passing through to look at the bats. Tourists visit the bigger cave roosts in Indonesia and Thailand too. Interestingly, the protection in the latter can be self-regulating. One tour guide took his party to the roost early and went inside to try to disturb the bats for a more spectacular emergence. The disturbance caused disruption for weeks afterwards and the other tour guides put matters right with a few well-chosen words to the offending guide.

Large fruit-bat camps in Australia, India, Indonesia and New Guinea are also now on the tourist trails. As well as the guides, local businesses all benefit from such bat-related tourism.

BAT WATCHING

Watching bats will provide many memorable experiences; joining one of the many bat watches organized by local bat groups is the easiest way to start. Although bats may be seen flying around any habitat at dusk, it is best to go where they gather in some numbers and can easily be seen in the afterglow of sunset. Lightly wooded edges of lakes are good places to see bats, and it is important to position yourself so the water is between you and the sunset. The brighter sky will reflect in the water and give you a better view of the bats.

Different species arrive to feed at different times, some will feed around the water's edge, some among the trees and others out over the water. Look out for the different ways the various species fly, some twisting and turning, some following direct paths, some high, others low.

When it is really dark, shine a spotlight across the water surface. This highlights the millions of insects on which the bats are feeding, and now and then a bat will fly into the beam. It is possible to illuminate with the beam a particularly large insect as it flies around for the last time and see a bat swoop down and catch it. You will gasp at the daring of the bats' aerobatics, experience the thrill of the chase as they feed, and be stunned by the skill of these remarkable flying mammals. If you can obtain a bat detector, then a wonderful evening becomes amazing and the exciting 'movies' suddenly acquire a sound-track.

EDUCATION

Generally information about bats is scarce and the little that does exist is often wrong (see box, *Myths exploded*, p.118). Many people have formed their main impression of bats from horror films, so it is hardly surprising that they develop false ideas about them. Bat conservation organizations around the world are now publishing more and more information about bats in books, in the media and on the Internet, and slowly the public perception is changing. Bats are becoming known as harmless, endangered creatures and certainly nothing to fear. Many bat conservation organizations have a junior wing, with publications aimed at the younger enthusiast. But conservationists

give talks in schools, and often the teacher learns as much as the students. Adult education is as important as that of the youngsters and educational talks on bats are now commonplace in many countries.

BATS AND THE LAW

Bats and their roosts have been given protection by law in most parts of the world to some degree. In Britain, for example, all bats and their roosts are protected, as are the feeding areas of some species. In the USA, the rarer species are protected across the continent and different states have their own laws, some protecting species at their roosts.

Enforcing the law is another matter, but having a law in place tells people that the leaders of their country believe that bats are worthy of protection. This is an important message to get across. Big businesses, local councils, religious authorities and government departments all have reputations to uphold, and they generally try to avoid breaking the laws regarding bats.

CAUSES OF DEATH

By far the biggest influence on bat populations results from human activities. Deforestation is killing off many thousands of individual bats and, in some cases, wiping out entire species. Even when some trees are left, they may be exposed to storms and blow over. The soil is soon washed away and the plants that sustain bats by providing insects or fruits can no longer grow. Roost sites are being chain-sawed away. The human impact on the landscape is now immense. Woodlands, fields and other habitats are dug up and replaced by roads and cities, and this affects the bats' feeding or roosting needs.

In the developed world, agriculture has been highly mechanized and insecticides are widely used to produce high crop-yields. Some of these poisons are ingested by bats and may affect their life expectancy or reproductive success. Researchers have evidence that these poisons can be laid down within the bats' bodies in the fat reserves used for winter hibernation, so that they act like ticking bombs. The bat survives only until it starts to burn up the fat.

Generally, there are far fewer insects around now than before the wide-scale use of these poisons, so there is less food for the bats. It is likely that the population crashes of free-tailed bats in Mexico were due to the introduction of these powerful modern insecticides into the ecosystem. In the UK such a pesticide (lindane) was widely used in attics to kill wood-boring beetles, and it was also found to kill any bat that came into contact with the treated timbers for at least two years after the spraying. Thousands of roofs were being treated annually, but now a safer pesticide (permethrin) is being used, due to the pressures of conservationists and the law. These are just some of the major indirect causes of deaths, but many others face bats.

DIRECT MORTALITY

Direct causes of death usually have less of an impact. Some native people eat bats as part of their traditional diet. With a stable human population, this is usually sustainable, but with modern influences on health, many populations of people

---

MYTHS EXPLODED

AS BLIND AS A BAT. Wrong. All bats have good eyesight, especially in dark conditions.

BATS FLY INTO YOUR HAIR. Wrong. Why would they want to? Microbats have such a superb echolocation system, they can easily see a single hair stretched in front of them and avoid it.

BATS IN THE BELFRY. Rarely true. Bats in churches are often in the nave or chancel. They do not like the noise of the bells, or the cold conditions and the pigeons. If the belfry is disused, however, then bats may move in.

BATS DRINK BLOOD. Most of the world's bats eat insects and fruits, and out of a total of almost 1,100 species only three species in tropical areas of the Americas take small amounts of blood.

Such false assumptions as those outlined above are constantly repeated around most of the world and, being rarely questioned, are often assumed to be true. No wonder people are nervous of bats if they are misled into thinking that they are blind, cannot see where they are going, will fly into their hair and then drink their blood!

are rising dramatically and the bats cannot cope with the greatly increased level of killing.

Natural predators of bats are few. Among the birds, there are some raptors that specialize in catching bats emerging at dusk and some opportunistic owls too. The bat falcon, *Falco rufigularis*, of the New World and the bat hawk, *Machaerhampus alcinus*, which occurs from Africa right across to New Guinea, wait outside cave roosts at dusk. Their agile flight enables them to catch emerging bats. Also waiting may be owls, but these are mostly more adept at catching ground mammals and insects flying more slowly and straighter than the bats.

Domestic cats can hear the high-frequency calls of bats and may lie in wait on a high roof for the bats to follow their usual flight path, then snatch them out of the air. Some snakes will lie in wait in the cave entrance and reach out to grab a passing meal. Locally, such predation can be devastating, as on the Pacific island of Guam, where the introduced brown tree snake, *Boiga irregularis*, has decimated bat populations.

Natural disasters occur, cave roofs collapse, caves flood, tree roosts blow over in the wind, weather patterns change so fruit or insects are not available at a time of need, hurricanes hit an island and strip it of fruit and cover. Individual bats miscalculate and get trapped on barbed wire, are knocked down by cars, hit power lines, fall into ponds or meet some other untimely end. They have been found floating in toilets, electrocuted in a light switch in a house under construction, caught in mouse traps,

BELOW Each month, local people on one of the Solomon Islands take about 1,000 small bats, in this case Dusky leaf-nosed bats, *Hipposideros ater*, as well as 100 fruit bats, for food all from just one cave.

ABOVE Bats have accidents, too. Some also get hooked up on thoughtlessly discarded fishing line hanging from trees.

impaled on car aerials, and drowned in water tanks in house roofs. In India it is sad to see the corpses of *Pteropus giganteus*, one of the largest species of flying foxes in the world, on the overhead power lines. They land on the top wire and swing down, just touching the bottom wire to conduct themselves into oblivion. Smaller bats hang up with impunity.

DISEASE

Disease can wipe out local populations of bats. Little is known about diseases afflicting bats, and few have yet been identified, but they are thought to have had a major effect on some of the fruit bat populations. Roosting colonially, the whole population is likely to be affected. The endemic Solomons flying fox, *Pteropus rayneri*, was surveyed in Choiseul in 1995 and its population was found to have decreased from 50,000 to 15,000 in just ten years. A disease thought to have been brought into the island by domestic animals was believed to be one of the main reasons for this serious population crash.

Estimates of over a million bats dying in winter hibernacula in the northeast USA since 2006 have been reported. All have fungus on their noses, and sometimes on their wings, so it has been dubbed 'white-nose syndrome' and is attributed to the snowy-white fungus, *Geomyces destructans*. The bats seem to arouse when infected, fly around, when they should be conserving energy, and so burn up stored fat and die from starvation. Extensive testing still has not determined how the fungus causes death nor has any cure been found. In the meantime tens of thousands of bats are dying each winter, principally the little brown bat, *Myotis lucifugus*. Presently the effects are restricted to this one area of the world. The fungus has been found on a few bats in Europe, but they have not died from it or any associated pathogens, nor have there been mass-deaths.

Glossary

CALCAR Spur of cartilage from the heel that supports the trailing edge of the tail membrane

CARNIVOROUS Meat eating

CHIROPTERA Latin name for bat ('hand wing')

DECIBEL A measure of sound volume

DOPPLER SHIFT The rise in frequency as an object approaches, and decrease as it moves away

DORSAL On the back

ECHOLOCATION Locating objects by listening for the echo of emitted sounds

ECTOTHERMIC Having low metabolic rate and use of external sources of heat to regulate body temperature (e.g. snakes)

ENDEMIC Present in a particular region

FAMILY Genera with similar characteristics

FOREARM LENGTH The length between the end of the elbow and wrist and used to give an indication of the overall size of a bat

FOSSIL Remains of animal or plant preserved in rocks

FRUGIVOROUS Fruit feeder

GENUS A group of species with similar characteristics

HETEROTHERMIC Regulating body temperatures to save energy consumption so able to stay warm, or cool down to ambient temperature (e.g. bats)

HIBERNACULUM A place where bats hibernate

HIBERNATE Passing the winter at a greatly reduced body temperature when the body mechanisms have slowed

HOMOEOTHERMIC Maintaining high body temperature at all times (e.g. humans)

INSECTIVOROUS Insect eating

INTERFEMORAL MEMBRANE Membrane of skin joining the back legs and often enclosing the tail

KHZ/KILOHERTZ Measure of frequency where one equals 1,000 cycles per second

LANCET Spike part of horseshoe bats' nose-leaf complex

LEK A gathering of displaying males

MEGACHIROPTERA 'Big bats', the Old World fruit bats

MICROCHIROPTERA 'Small bats', the insectivorous bats

MIST NET A fine net stretched between two poles used for catching bats

MOLAR Flat teeth at the back of the mouth used for grinding

NIGHT ROOST Resting place used at night to eat captured food, digest previously captured food, rest or socialize

NOSE-LEAF Skin or fleshy shapes around the nostrils linked to echolocation

ORDER A grouping of families in classification

PLAGIOPATAGIUM Membrane of skin on the wing between the fifth finger, the forearm, the body and the leg

PROPATAGIUM Part of the wing membrane in front of the forearm, from the thumb to the body

ROOST The place where bats shelter, rest and breed, and also used to describe a collection of bats

SELLA Central part of the horseshoe bats' nose-leaf complex, sideways flattened

SEXUAL DIMORPHISM Difference between appearance of males and females, e.g. male microbats are smaller than females

SPECIES A population that can interbreed to produce fertile offspring

TEMPERATE Mid-latitude climatic zone, often with very cold winters

TORPOR A lowering of body temperature by reducing metabolic rate so saving energy, usually at higher temperature than hibernation

TRAGUS A projection made of cartilage which stands up inside the front of the ear

ULTRASOUND Sounds with frequency above that which humans can hear

VENTRAL Underside

Further information

FURTHER READING

Australian Bats, Sue Churchill. Reed New Holland, 1998.

A World List of Mammalian Species, G.B. Corbet and J.F. Hill. Oxford University Press, 3rd edn, 1991.

Bats, M. Brock Fenton. Facts on File, 1992.

Bats, Phil Richardson. Whittet Books, 2nd edn., 2000.

Bats Biology and Behaviour, John D. Altringham. Oxford University Press, 1996.

Bats in Question: The Smithsonian Answer Book, Don E. Wilson and Merlin D. Tuttle. Smithsonian Institution Press, 1997.

Microchiropteran Bats, Global Status Survey and Conservation Action Plan, Simon P. Mickleburgh, Anthony M. Hutson and Paul A. Racey. IUCN, 2001.

Old World Fruit Bats, Simon P. Mickleburgh, Anthony M. Hutson and Paul A. Racey. IUCN, 1992.

The Bat House Builder's Book, Merlin D. Tuttle & Donna L. Hensley. Bat Conservation International, 1993.

Walker's Bats of the World, Ronald M. Novak. The Johns Hopkins University Press, 1994.

INTERNET RESOURCES

NB. Web addresses are subject to change

http://www.batcall.csu.edu.au/abs/absmain.htm

[Details of the Australasian Bat Society, conservation issues, conference details, bat species, resources and latest news.]

http://www.batcon.org

Bat Conservation International, PO Box 162603, Austin, Texas 78716, USA

[Outlines the operation of the US Bat Conservation International with latest news and press releases, publications, resources, information for students and teachers and good links to other bat websites.]

http://www.bats.org.uk

The Bat Conservation Trust, 15 Cloisters House, 8 Battersea Park Road, London SW8 4BG, UK

[Describes the UK Bat Conservation Trust, provides information about UK species, their protection and distribution. Includes details of surveys underway, bat detectors and contact details.]

http://www.eurobats.org

[About bat conservation in Europe, training opportunities, conference details and events. Mostly linked to the European laws involving bats.]

http://www.fledermaus-dietz.de/publications.html

[Field guide to European species with photographs.]

PICTURE CREDITS

p.4 © Jouan & Rius/naturepl.com; p.6 © Craig K. Lorenz/Science Photo Library; p.7 left and right © Phil Richardson; p.10 Ray Burrows/© NHM; p.11 © Dietmar Nill/BBC Natural History Unit; p.12 Illustrated Image/© NHM; p.13 top © Phil Richardson; p.13 bottom Mike Eaton/© NHM; p.14 top © John Altringham; pp.15, 18 top and bottom, 20, 21 left © Phil Richardson; p.21 right © Bryan Brown; p22 top, bottom © Phil Richardson; p.24 © E. Bowen-Jones/FFI; p.25 © Dietmar Nill/BBC Natural History Unit; p.26 left and right © John Altringham; p.27 Mike Eaton/© NHM; p.28 © Michele Westmorlan/naturepl.com; p.30 © Morten Strange/NHPA; p.31 © Carol Buchanan/RSPCA Photolibrary; p.32 © Michael Pitts/BBC Natural History Unit; p.34 © Phil Richardson; p.35 © Hugh Maynard/BBC Natural History Unit; p.36 © Jim Clare/ BBC Natural History Unit; p.37 © Dietmar Nill/BBC Natural History Unit; p.40 © L Hugh Newman/NHPA; p.41© John Altringham; p.42 © Phil Richardson; p.44 © Pete Oxford/naturepl.com; p.46 © Phil Richardson; p.47 © Daniel Heuclin/NHPA; pp.48, 49 top, 50 © Phil Richardson; p.52 © Anup Shah/BBC Natural History Unit; p.55 © NHPA/Photoshot; p.56 © Melvin Grey/NHPA; p.57 © Pete Oxford/BBC Natural History Unit; p.58 left and right © Phil Richardson; p.59 © Merlin D Tuttle, Bat Conservation International; p.60 © Phil Richardson; p.61 © Merlin D Tuttle, Bat Conservation International; pp.62, 64 © Phil Richardson; pp.65, 66 © Merlin D Tuttle, Bat Conservation International; p.67 © ANT Photo Library/NHPA; p.69 © Stephen Dalton/NHPA; p.70 © Melvin Grey/NHPA; p.72 © Stephen Dalton/NHPA; p.73 © E. Bowen-Jones/ Choiseul '95; p.74 © A.N.T./NHPA; pp.75-79 © Phil Richardson; p.80 © Merlin D Tuttle, Bat Conservation International; p.81 © Phil Richardson; p.82 © Tim Martin/BBC Natural History Unit; p.83 © E. Bowen-Jones/FFI; p.84 left © E. Bowen-Jones/FFI; p.84 right © Dietmar Nill/BBC Natural History Unit; p.85 © T Martin/RSPCA; p.86 © Stephen Dalton/NHPA; p.88 © Dave Watts/naturepl.com; p.90 © Phil Richardson; p.91 © NHPA/Photoshot; p.92 © Phil Richardson; p.93 © © NHPA/Photoshot; p.95 © Stephen Krasemann/ NHPA Photolibrary; p.96 top © Phil Richardson; p.96 bottom © The Bat Conservation Trust; pp.97, 98 © Phil Richardson; p.99 © Phil Savoie/BBC Natural History Unit; p.101 © Phil Richardson; p.102 © Stephen Dalton/NHPA; p.103 © Colin Seddon/RSPCA Photolibrary; p.104 © Phil Savoie/BBC Natural History Unit; pp.105, 106 © Phil Richardson; p.108 © © Inaki Relanzon/naturepl.com; p.109 © Daniel Heuclin/NHPA; p.111 left © Mike Eaton/© NHM; p.111 right © Mark Hamblin/RSPCA Photolibrary; pp.113 to 120 Phil Richardson.

All other images are copyright of the Natural History Museum, London.

Index